SWIFT CARAVANS

ANDREW JENKINSON

AMBERLEY

This book is dedicated to Ken, Joan and Peter Smith.

First published 2018

Amberley Publishing
The Hill, Stroud,
Gloucestershire, GL5 4EP

www.amberley-books.com

Copyright © Andrew Jenkinson, 2018

The right of Andrew Jenkinson to be identified as the Author
of this work has been asserted in accordance with the
Copyright, Designs and Patents Act 1988.

All rights reserved. No part of this book may be reprinted
or reproduced or utilised in any form or by any electronic,
mechanical or other means, now known or hereafter invented,
including photocopying and recording, or in any information
storage or retrieval system, without the permission in writing
from the Publishers.

Map illustration by Thomas Bohm, User Design, Illustration and Typesetting.

ISBN: 978 1 4456 5887 2 (print)
ISBN: 978 1 4456 5888 9 (ebook)

British Library Cataloguing in Publication Data.
A catalogue record for this book is available from the British Library.

Typeset in 10pt on 13pt Celeste.
Origination by Amberley Publishing.
Printed in the UK.

Contents

	Foreword	4
Chapter One	In the Beginning – 1964 to 1969	6
Chapter Two	New Production Plant and Expanding Markets – 1970 to 1979	23
Chapter Three	The '80s: New Designs and Developments – 1980 to 1989	42
Chapter Four	Swift Expands its Brand Portfolio – 1990 to 1999	58
Chapter Five	Expansion, Holiday Homes and Advances in Construction Technology – 2000 to 2018	73

Foreword

The author stands with the Swift 50th Anniversary display at the NEC in 2014.

Back in mid-1969, when I just a young boy, my parents purchased their first touring caravan. No strangers to caravanning, my grandparents had begun in the mid-1950s, and had purchased a new Sprite Musketeer by the early '60s. From those early days I had an interest in the UK caravan industry, and from about the age of eleven I watched as new manufacturers came and went. I first noticed Swift in 1969, when caravanning friends of my parents had bought a new 1969 Swift Danette. I remember being intrigued by its triple front and rear window design and its spacious interior.

I remember watching the Swift company progress and become very popular, especially among discerning rally goers. 'Stable towing' and 'quality finish' were words often used to describe the Swift range. In poor economic times the caravan trade could be hit hard, but Swift provided the right caravan at the right price and weight. By the 1980s Swift really shone, with some great designs such as the Cottingham, Challenger and the Corniche with aerodynamic profiles and rear roof spoilers.

I couldn't have foreseen their rapid expansion and takeovers, which surprised me over the years! However, Peter Smith (son of founder Ken Smith) would be shrewd; with go-ahead thinking, he knew exactly where he wanted Swift to be, and that was as the UK's number one leisure vehicle manufacturer.

I wonder what Ken Smith would have thought of his company's achievements and of how Swift has become a well-known brand in caravanning/motorhome and holiday home circles. I imagine that he would be proud of not just the Swift name, but of Peter too, for carrying on in often difficult times and expanding the company on the good foundations he laid back in 1964 at the workshop in Hull on Hedon Road.

CHAPTER ONE

In the Beginning – 1964 to 1969

After the Second World War, the UK would see many changes. Cars were sold in greater numbers as a new consumer boom would begin and by the 1950s holidays had also became more affordable, with many families seeing the touring caravan as a great way to get away for weekends as well as longer breaks. As caravanning became more popular by the end of the '50s, a UK caravan manufacturing industry was thriving, exporting most of its production into Europe. However, it would be the next decade, the 1960s, that would see further increases in caravan ownership and manufacturing. With an increase of caravan sites becoming available and new family cars being launched, such as the Ford Cortina and Austin/Morris 1100s, caravanning saw more families than ever choose this way of holidaying. It was the beginning of this decade that would see Hull develop as a major force in Europe as a producer of touring and holiday home caravans.

Willerby Caravans, who began manufacturing caravans from 1946 at Willerby, near Hull, founded this area in East Yorkshire as a caravan-manufacturing hot spot. Some employees left Willerby in the late '50s to begin caravan manufacturing in the surrounding parts of Hull and the '60s would see an almost epidemic scale of new caravan manufactures start up. Companies producing caravans were appearing on a monthly basis in the area and although other parts of the UK also saw new caravan names appearing, Hull was to prove the nucleus of such expansion.

This is where the story of Swift Caravans begins. In 1964, Ken Smith, a qualified sheet metal worker and wood machinist operator, had been previously hiring out washing machines as a business. Utilising his skills, he set up another business in a small workshop in Hull, making sheds, greenhouses and garages. The new business was relatively successful, but Ken was to look at another avenue in which the potential was even greater. By this time several Hull manufacturers had begun: Ace, Mardon, Robin, Lissett, Alpine, Coachcraft, Astral, Silverline and also Welton, who were on the outskirts at Welton village.

In a workshop near his, Ken Smith had noticed a small touring caravan being built. The builder of this touring caravan was Ken Day. Day, a joiner, had worked briefly for a relatively new small company, Ace Caravans, with its founder, Terry Reed. The two Kens decided that they could both manufacture caravans as a joint venture. With a capital of £100, the premises were based at 1539 Hedon Road, Hull. In the late summer, the first

The 1960s and early '70s witnessed UK-built tourers being exported in big numbers.

In 1946, Willerby began manufacturing caravans, and established Hull as the hub of this industry.

Astral was just one of several new Hull-based manufacturers, along with Swift, in the early 1960s.

Swift Caravans Ltd. Regd. January 1. 1539 Hedon Road, Hull. To take over the business of the manufacture of caravans and associated parts of steel and wooden constructions, general engineers and woodwork manufacturers carried on at Hull by K. Smith and K. W. Day, etc. Nominal capital : £100 in £1 shares. Permanent directors : Kenneth Smith, 95 Tweendykes Road, Sutton, Hull, and Kenneth Day, 1 Hastings Road, Thorngumbald.

The seeds of Swift were sown in mid-1964.

A Swift Clubman Ten 1964/5, having been restored by Swift.

Ten's interior; a family model, it slept four.

branded Swift caravan was built, simply being named the Swift Ten. A four-berth 3.2-m tourer, it came with an end kitchen. The dinette was situated at the front end and included a lino floor, a two-burner hob and grill, a sink and (plastic) drainer, as well as a hand-operated Whale pump to feed the sink. For £289, the Swift was marketed at the middle-price sector and was aimed at the family who owned such cars as the Austin/Morris 1100.

Towards the end of 1964, for the 1965 model year, Swift had added two more models, both of which were four berth: the Clubman and the Valken. The caravans of the three-model range were priced at £289, £369 and £445, being aimed very much at the mid-market.

Ken Day had decided to move on, leaving Ken Smith to buy his share of the company, and by early 1965 Ken and his wife Joan were the owners of Swift Caravans. Although caravan sales were in general booming, with the amount of manufacturers appearing,

SWIFT

A NEW NAME FAST SETTING HIGH STANDARDS IN QUALITY AND WORKMANSHIP

Straight from the manufacturing heart of Britain's caravan industry comes a new name, SWIFT CARAVANS. Already in a few short months there has been a big demand for the exciting SWIFT tourers, so make sure you see these sparkling new models at your nearest distributors before deciding on your new caravan.

Write for full details and address of your nearest stockists.

SWIFT CLUBMAN	10'	£289 ex. works
SWIFT CLUBMAN	13' (illus.)	£369 ,,
SWIFT CLUBMAN	15'	£445 ,,

SWIFT CLUBMAN 13'

GO **SWIFT** AND BE **SURE!**

TRADE ENQUIRIES INVITED

WRITE TO

SWIFT CARAVANS LTD 1539 HEDON ROAD, HULL   TEL. HULL 74251

The first Swift advert from early 1965.

1966 ELDDIS 10 ft.

Elddis began in 1965 and was one of Swift's early competitors from this era.

times were tough. At one stage the buyout Ken Smith's finances became stretched, and it was touch and go whether the Swift brand would be able to continue.

Ken Smith knew that if he could establish quality caravans at the right price, Swift had a future. With steady sales and a few limited staff, Ken would deliver caravans on his 'days off', essentially working seven days a week. Swift was a tiny player compared to manufacturers of this period such as Astral, Thomson and of course the Ci Group, and a never-ending stream of new manufacturers like Elddis made for a very competitive marketplace.

Swift were still basically an unknown maker, but word of mouth and hard graft would begin to slowly pay off. With a steady increase in dealers, demand went up, and the original 100 foot x 40 foot shed used for the first Swift factory was expanded to keep up. The extra factory building was erected by Ken and some of his employees, which helped to keep costs down. The Smiths had eight employees in 1966 and anybody with a tow bar fitted to their car was often asked to deliver caravans on their days off!

An aerial view of Swift's factory from around 1967/8.

A whole new rethink to the Swift profile was implemented by 1966. This year would see the start of using the 'Ette' names for all new models produced and Alouette, Silhouette and Baronette joined the existing model names. The Smiths' family home was detached and had a large front-lawned garden area. The early days witnessed the new Swifts in the mid- to late '60s on display with a small marquee, with Joan providing tea and cakes to visiting dealers. Costs were always watched, so saving money where possible was a priority in these early days. Their son Peter was now also involved with the company. During the school holidays, Peter would help his dad in the factory by doing various jobs – a good foundation for running the company later on.

Ken Smith was seeing interest from Europe, where UK caravans were popular and had a large share of the growing market. By 1966/7, Swifts were being shipped out to West Germany and Denmark in what would be the start of the Swift name becoming a main exporter to Europe and beyond many years later. Within a few years, Ken had built up a trust with suppliers, who in hard times would waiver payment dates, knowing that they

The SWIFT BARONETTE 13' B.W.
13' x 6' 9" 4 BERTH - OPTIONAL 5 BERTH AT EXTRA COST
END KITCHEN AND TOILET - 12cwt. u.w.

Swift's 1966 Baronette had one of the successful family layouts.

The Smiths' house and gardens played host to the new models for some years.

Taken in summer 1969, the 1970 range is displayed.

Swift's 1970 line-up on the Smiths lawn for prospective dealers to view.

Ken Smith with son Peter (left), getting ready for the trade show.

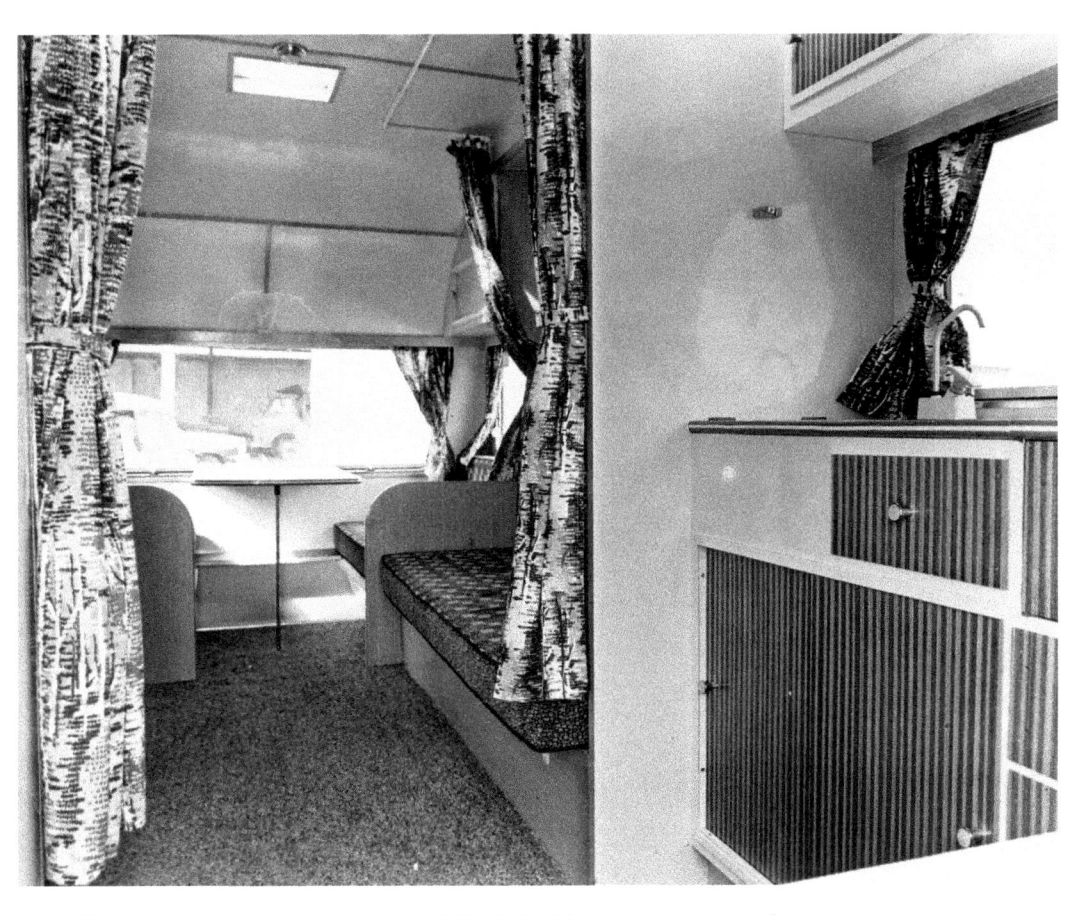

The interior of a 1967 export model. Swift had begun to export early on.

would always receive it. Peak Trailers was one such supplier, which would be the firm foundation of the Swift tourers.

Swifts were built on Peak steel chassis from the start but back then they weren't galvanised or treated so they had to be spray painted, with owners having to carry out the procedure every few years! Swift tourers would be fully insulated and came with gas lighting and used real wood veneers. The Swifts were seen as a quality caravan for the Clubman market and the Swift became known as the Flying Clubman Series. Swift were gaining more dealers but still encountered strong competition. Ken Smith knew there would be no let up on hard work.

The 1960s and '70s saw the Earls Court Caravan Show as the main exhibition where manufacturers had the chance to show the caravan world their latest models. Crowds of 180,000 plus visitors attended the ten-day show in November, with orders for millions of pounds being taken from home and abroad. Getting a stand was not easy, with the expanding caravan industry taking up the available space, and it was also expensive to exhibit. However, by 1967 Swift had a stand at the show. This was an ideal opportunity for Swift to showcase their new, redesigned and distinctive-looking 1968 tourers.

Peak chassis were the foundations of Swift's tourers.

The interior of the 1966 Swift Silhouette. This family van cost £357.

The SWIFT SILHOUETTE 11′ 6″

11′ 6″ x 6′ 6″ - 4 BERTH - CENTRE KITCHEN AND TOILET
12¼ cwt. u.w.

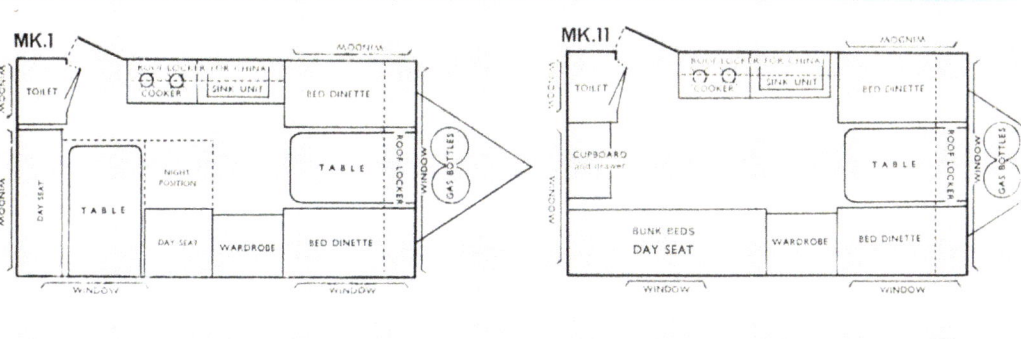

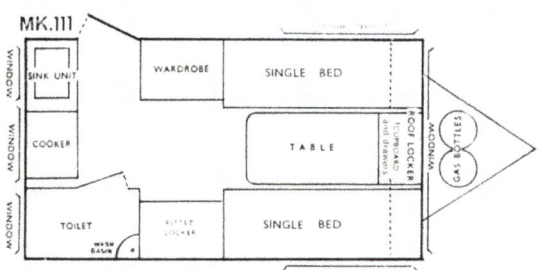

Seven pole wiring with one interior electric light, two gas lights, griller cooker, sink, water pump, front large roof lockers, locker fitted for crockery, fitted carpet, doors and drawers positive locking, foam bedding, Afromosia furniture, gas bottle holder, hook on tables, dividing curtain, toilet compartment, all alum 22 gauge, choice of colour scheme. Fitted personalised mud flaps.

Swift's Silhouette Mk 2 from 1967 sported a large front stone guard and a glazed stable door.

The 1968 Swift profile. With triple front windows, the Swift look was born.

Prior to having a stand, Ken Smith would conduct business in the Alpine bar near Earls Court, which would be visited by dealers, manufacturers and suppliers. Ken would spend hours in the smokey bar with potential dealers. Once an interest was shown, Peter was instructed to take the customer on the Underground to Swift-dealers Venture Caravans, who had a full display of the Swifts. As soon as Peter had done his 'salesmanship', he would then bring them back to the show!

Once the company had a stand at the show, this made selling and exhibiting the models far easier. In those days Peter and his dad used to put down their own floor covering of lino on the stand. When the show was over it was taken back to the factory and used for the caravans! Peter told me once, 'If some owners had lifted up the carpet in their Swift in those days they may have noticed the odd cigarette burn in the pattern!' Back then, Swift did very little in the way of advertising, but with a vast market to tap into Ken saw the benefits of reaching a wider audience.

By 1968 Swift advertisements were appearing in various caravan magazine publications and along with these Swift caravans were also receiving excellent reviews from various editorial tests. The 1968 profile of the Swift had added three deep windows at the front and the rear, while a large unpainted stucco piece of aluminium was placed at the front to stop stones from denting the aluminium. The deep triple windows at both front and rear gave most tow car drivers perfect 'see-through vision', allowing them to see the traffic behind them at all times. It became a feature of Swifts over the years and a selling point too.

The year 1968 also saw two new models introduced. The first was the Rapide, which had an 8-foot 6-inch-long body with a width of just 6 foot 4 inches and weighed in at 458 kg. Designed for the BMC Mini or other small cars, the Rapide would be in production until 1971. The Coronette had the same floor plan as the Rapide but in a longer 10-foot body.

SWIFT CARAVANS present the Coronette

together with their complete range of fast Touring Models—tested in all Continental Countries. Designed with low line safety see through vision—even with a Mini car. See and test tow them at your nearest agent; also ask to see the De-luxe 2-berth "Silhouette" and "Alouette" models.

Please contact your nearest agents as listed.

SWIFT CARAVANS

SOMERDEN ROAD, HEDON ROAD, HULL
Telephone: OHU2 74251

Above: Swift's new Coronette from 1968 – a 10-foot four berth.

Right: Swift boasted 'see-through vision' – a must-have for caravanners back then.

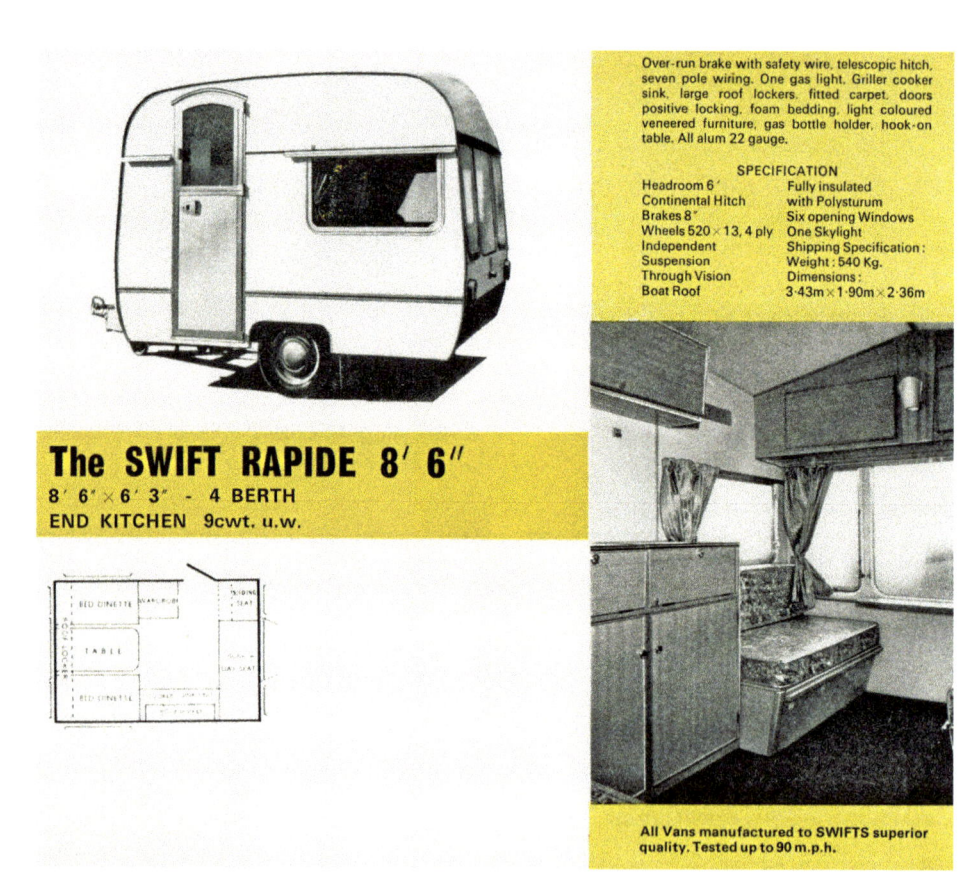

The SWIFT RAPIDE 8' 6"
8' 6" × 6' 3" – 4 BERTH
END KITCHEN 9cwt. u.w.

Over-run brake with safety wire, telescopic hitch, seven pole wiring. One gas light. Griller cooker sink, large roof lockers, fitted carpet, doors positive locking, foam bedding, light coloured veneered furniture, gas bottle holder, hook-on table. All alum 22 gauge.

SPECIFICATION
Headroom 6'
Continental Hitch
Brakes 8"
Wheels 520 × 13, 4 ply
Independent Suspension
Through Vision
Boat Roof
Fully insulated with Polysturum
Six opening Windows
One Skylight
Shipping Specification:
Weight: 540 Kg.
Dimensions:
3·43m × 1·90m × 2·36m

All Vans manufactured to SWIFTS superior quality. Tested up to 90 m.p.h.

The micro 8-foot 6-inch Rapide four berth was designed for the Mini car.

Sleeping four, neither models featured washrooms, but back then that was the norm for this size and family layout.

As the 1960s came to a close, Swift added what was originally intended as an export-only model for the Danish market to the UK after popular demand. Named the Danette it had a centre toilet room and kitchen with a rear single dinette. Four berth, the front could be made into a large bed that would sleep three! By 1969, Swift also added an underfloor cool food box and foot-operated Whale water pump to all caravans in the range. Interiors were also brighter, while furniture was finished in Afrormosia. The Swifts had found their identity and were gaining a loyal following among keen caravanners.

The early years had begun hard, but with drive and determination from the off, Ken Smith, with the help of wife Joan and son Peter, had grown the company significantly in five years. From an unknown range of tourers in an ever-crowded marketplace, Swift had found their identity and had earned a reputation as a producer of stable towing tourers with a quality finish. Production had also risen to 400 units a year with a workforce of around twenty-five, and the factory was now over 10,000 square feet as opposed to the 4,000 square feet of 1964/5. The next decade would be one of mixed fortunes for the Smith family, both on a personal level as well as a business one.

Seven pole wiring with one gas light, griller cooker, sink, water pump, front large roof lockers, locker fitted for crockery, fitted carpet, doors and drawers positive locking, foam bedding, afromosia furniture, gas bottle holder, hook-on tables. All alum 22 gauge.

SPECIFICATION

Headroom 6'
Telescopic Hitch
Brakes 8"
Wheels 520 × 13, 4 ply
Independent Suspension
Through Vision
Boat Roof
Fully insulated with Polysturum

Six opening Windows
One Skylight
Over-run Brakes with Safety Wire
Shipping Specification:
Weight: 600 Kgs.
Dimensions:
3·80m × 1·90m × 2·36m

The SWIFT CORONETTE 10'
10' × 6' 3" - 4 BERTH
CENTRE KITCHEN 10cwt. u.w.

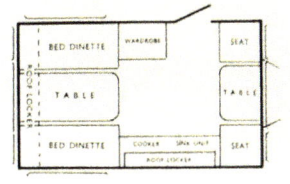

A Coronette export model from 1968.

1969 saw the Swift profile tweaked – this was the export Danette.

SWIFT CARAVANS
Somerdon Road, Hull, Yorks.

	Length	Width	Berths	Weight (cwt.)	Price
Baronette	13ft.	6ft. 9in.	4	13	£459
Silhouette	11ft. 9in.	6ft. 6in.	4	12	£429
Silhouette	11ft. 9in.	6ft. 6in.	2	12	£459
Alouette	10ft. 9in.	6ft. 6in.	4	11	£386
Alouette	10ft. 9in.	6ft. 6in.	2	11	£398
Coronette	10ft.	6ft. 3in.	4	10	£358
Rapide	8ft. 9in.	6ft. 3in.	4	9	£319

The Swift 1969 line-up. Pictured is the 13-foot Baronette.

Chapter Two

New Production Plant and Expanding Markets – 1970 to 1979

The 1960s had at times proved tough for the Smith family, with Ken working constantly to develop his touring range of Swift caravans. With his wife Joan and son Peter, the next decade promised more growth. Just a few years previously, in 1968, the Swift profile with its triple front and rear windows had been established. Ken now wanted to evolve the Swift look and also keep interiors traditional and appealing to clubman buyers. The '70s would present new challenges but the beginning of the decade would continue to see caravans

Swift was still seeing new tourer makes appearing, such as the Lunar in mid-1969.

For 1970 Ken Smith gave the caravans green lower side panels, making the Swifts more distinctive.

in high demand. New manufacturers were still cropping up, such as Lunar, Buccaneer, Beverley Coachcraft and the merger of Ace Caravans with holiday-home-makers Belmont Caravans in 1972 to form Ace Belmont International.

For 1970, the plain white exterior was to change. The new range would sport a pale green lower side panel, breaking up the all-white exterior finish. Ken had looked at the possibility of Swift using one-piece aluminium side panels, which would then be glued to the body framing. This idea wasn't to be implemented and the Swifts would continue to be built using the traditional coachbuilt method for another twelve years. Each Swift sold came with a handbook. By today's standards it was primitive but the information given at the time was all that was needed – it even came with Caravanning Code rules!

Six models would be produced for the 1970 season with the 15-foot Corvette being dropped, before returning for 1972. Two layout options, with the 11-foot 6-inch Silhouette and 10-foot Alouette, increased the layout choices to eight. Swift would offer two furniture wood finishes for the 1970 season; this was either in light Italian ash or dark afrormosia. On the extras list you could have an Electrolux fridge (£38), a full oven (£20) and a floor-mounted gas point (£3) to attach a gas fire to. In 1970 the most expensive Swift was the new five-berth 14-foot Danette at £521, while the cheapest was the Rapide at £340, which could sleep four.

The interior of the 1970 Swift Danette – a then-new five berth.

The early Swift handbook even had advice on caravanning!

Swift had, as already mentioned, built up a good relationship with its suppliers, such as Ellbee who supplied doors and windows, plus Peak Trailers. Peak would give Swift extended credit, which helped the company enormously in this period. The new decade witnessed increased dealerships, which now totalled thirty-four, and these helped keep sales buoyant. With exports playing a large part in sales, the Hedon Road factory was now deemed not large enough to cope with the increase in demand.

The solution was to find a new factory that would also have room to expand further should the need arise. A new site was found near the village of Cottingham, on the outskirts of Hull. By August 1970 the company had moved to its new production area, which was based on Dunswell Road. The new factory was 15,000 square feet – a third larger than the old factory. The number of employees increased too; from the handful employed a few years earlier, the company now had around thirty members of staff, which increased further to around fifty.

Swift's new factory was geared up to produce more tourers, while maintaining quality at the same time. The new factory was surrounded by open land that was ideal for storage. With the 1971 season, Swift altered the furniture finish to a light oak effect and changed the upholstery too, plus they now had just five models in the line-up. Swift also decided to make the three front windows non-opening. Along with other manufacturers of touring caravans of that period, Swift had experienced water entering in through the front seals in heavy, driving rain. By making them non-opening, this eradicated the problem.

It was in this period that the next milestone in Swift's history took place. In early 1971 a notice was placed in the UK's leading caravan magazine, *Practical Caravan*. It asked for

Swift's new Cottingham factory enabled production to be stepped up by 1971, allowing further expansion over the coming decade.

The Cottingham factory had more storage. Peter Smith inspects the latest batch of Swifts before dispatch.

The Dunswell Road factory had land to store these new 1975 Swifts.

any interested Swift owners wanting to form a club to contact a Mr R. Goddard. With over forty replies, Swift's new owners club was established with an inaugural rally at the end of August 1971. It was held at Alton Towers, where twenty-eight Swift tourers turned up for the event. From this first meet, the Swift Owners Club (www.swift-owners-club.com) would grow further in numbers and in rallies.

Even a factory rally was held at the Dunswell Road premises in June 1972, which involved viewing the 1973 prototypes, and in 1974 the Owners Club had its first continental rally, which was held at an RAF station in Berlin. After forty-plus years, the Swift Owners Club now takes all the Swift-owned brands, including motorhomes too. The club would also go on to raise thousands of pounds for numerous charities through various rally events.

By 1972 the Swift range would receive a new model, the Corvette – a 14-foot family tourer priced at £590. Production of the tiny Rapide was to be stopped while all the other Swifts would see some upgrades. These included a stainless steel sink replacing the plastic unit and new locker doors, as well as new ceiling and side wall coverings. With the new factory now well and truly up and running, and with sales witnessing further increases, 1972 should have been a time to celebrate.

Right: A Swift owners club was established in August 1971.

Below: Swift's Corvette was based on its export layout. This model proved a top seller from launch in 1972.

Swift was now firmly established, with various caravan magazines singing the praises of Swift tourers. In March of 1973, VAT at 10 per cent was to be added to all touring caravans. With higher inflation and the oil crisis, prices of caravans in general rose considerably. The economy went into a general slowdown, but Swift still had orders slowly coming in. Inevitably, caravan manufacturers had to cut production, and even the larger concerns were not immune from lay-offs. With Swift's good line-up of tourers for 1973, they were well prepared for the harder year ahead.

At the 1972 Earls Court Show, Swift displayed their latest 1973 models. The Alouette models were dropped, leaving a range of just four top-selling Swifts. Swift left interiors unchanged apart from upgrading the soft furnishings, which helped keep costs down. At the show, an official handover of a Danette to the actress Nicola Pagett for the National Society for Mentally Handicapped Children took place; the caravan being a gift for the Society to use for holidays. Swift as a company would go on to support many charities over the years.

The Earls Court Show proved a success, and Ken was pleased with the growing popularity of Swift Caravans. The hard work was paying off. The Smiths knew, however, that 1973 would be tough for the industry as a whole, but Swift was growing. Then, just eleven days after the 1972 Earls Court Show had finished, there was a family tragedy. Ken Smith died suddenly on 28 November 1972, aged just fifty-six. The shock of Ken's sudden passing meant that Joan and Peter not only had to deal with their grief, but also had to keep the business running. Ken had been a keen caravanner and had used his experiences with his family to create the practical touches incorporated in all the Swift models; his experience was going to be greatly missed.

Peter, along with mum Joan, knew that all the hard work that Ken had carried out, and in some ways had possibly affected his health, had to be continued. Peter was now in the MD seat and had the responsibility of running and expanding the company, just as his dad had done. Peter would build up a strong team around him over the years with names such as Ron Shipp and David Rochester, and, later, Richard White and Tony Hailey; Peter could then concentrate on new ideas and models, being very hands-on in his work.

In the mid-1970s the British Caravan Road Rally was in its twentieth year and attracted novices and professionals alike. Dealers, manufacturers and suppliers took part in road rallying with caravan in tow, with a race track section being added for the 1973 event. Peter, along with then Swift dealers Goodall's, entered a Swift Silhouette with great results, winning first overall, fourth in the special sections and first in the track and road section using a Triumph 2000 estate tow car. This proved Swift's durability, sturdy construction and towing qualities. Over the years Peter would be successful in this field, with Swift always collecting trophies.

The mid-1970s would see Swift being prominent in other caravan rallies, proving their stability on the road. Peter was and still is keen in rallying and his son, Guy, also became involved in motorsport by the early '80s. Having a successful career in motor racing as part of team Bentley, Swift would supply motorhomes for his racing seasons over the years. The British Caravan & Yorkshire Road Rally involved towing caravans over some of the roughest roads and quickly around tracks, with the caravans often being written off in the process. This event gave Swift further exposure and as Peter Smith later said: 'It was great

At Earls Court in 1972, Ken and Joan Smith presented a Swift Danette to television actress Nicola Pagett for charity. Sadly, Ken died not long after this photo was taken.

Peter Smith at the wheel of the Datsun and Swift outfit. Caravan road rallying was popular for years and Swift got heavily involved.

Peter Smith rallying again with a Hillman Avenger and a 1971 Swift Rapide in the background.

32

Rallying was intense, with both dealers and suppliers backing the Swift team.

Peter Smith looking happy with his driving performance in around 1974.

Active participation in Caravan Road Rallies over recent years have shown that the stresses placed on a caravan are far in excess of a normal lifetimes wear, but the knowledge gained has been incorporated into normal production models to produce a range of caravans with reliability second to none. The proof of this being that during 1976 Swift Caravans have taken the team award from the last four rallies.

Team Awards 1976

1st Lombard/Caravan Club International Road Rally
1st Severnwye Road Rally
1st Yorkshire Road Rally
1st Red Rose Road Rally

Individual Awards

1st	1973	Yorkshire Road Rally
2nd	1975	Yorkshire Road Rally
1st	1976	Yorkshire Road Rally
2nd	1976	Yorkshire Road Rally
3rd	1976	Yorkshire Road Rally
2nd	1975	Severnwye Road Rally
2nd	1976	Severnwye Road Rally
3rd	1976	Severnwye Road Rally
2nd	1975	Heart of England
2nd	1976	Heart of England
3rd	1976	Heart of England
1st	1976	'Caravan' Rally Championship
2nd	1976	'Caravan' Rally Championship

The list of rallying achievements by Swift from 1973 was impressive.

fun and was a popular event with caravanners – it also helped to improve the construction of the caravan too!'

By 1974 Swift would also prove how well their caravans towed, being very economical in the process. With fuel prices rising, Peter set out to prove that Swifts used less fuel when towing compared to competitors' models. Using a Hillman Avenger family saloon with a Silhouette in tow, 60 miles was covered with an average consumption of 27.45 mpg. The figure recorded when the car was driven over the same route solo was only 7 miles less, verifying Swift's efficiency.

For the 1974 season Swift introduced a new model, the Pirouette; a 13-foot 6-inch-long family model based on the popular Danette layout but in a smaller shell. The Pirouette was to become another long-running Swift model for the company. Meanwhile, the 1974 models were now equipped with electric water pumps to the kitchen (cold only), while the washroom had a manual pump. 12 volt striplights were added to compliment the gas lights while kitchens were also given an integrated stainless steel hotplate and sink. Soft

Swift CARAVANS FOR THE ECONOMY RUN

MORE MILES TO THE GALLON WHEN TOWING A SWIFT TOURER

Swift's economy tow in 1974 set out to prove towing a Swift didn't mean big fuel bills.

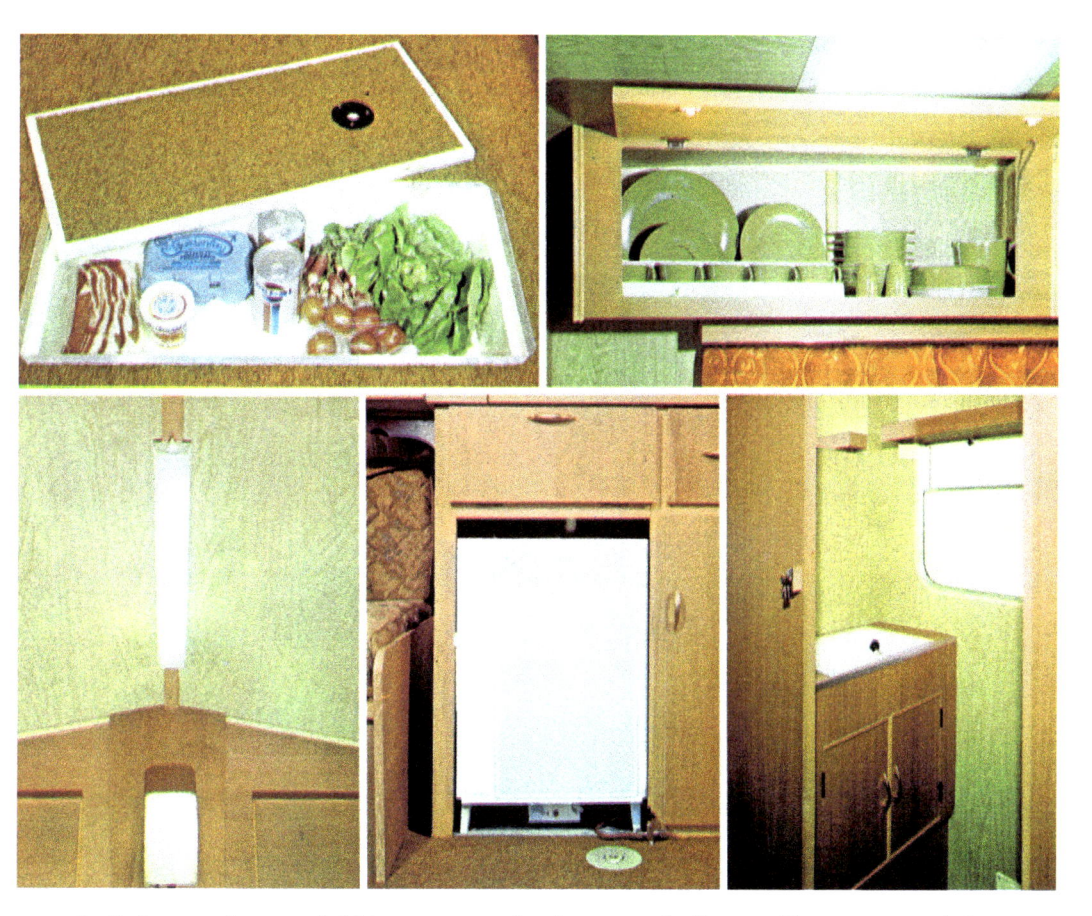

Swift features for 1974. A fridge was an option, but an underfloor cool box was enough for some.

35

The Swift Doublette, launched for 1975, was a hit with couples.

In 1976 Swift launched its up-market Corniche 14/5 model.

furnishings were changed but all Swifts now came with a drawbar shroud and front gas bottle locker too. This further enhanced the 'Swift look'.

From the mid-1970s, Peter Smith further pushed the Swift line-up by introducing a new couple's model, the Doublette, in 1975. This was followed in 1976 by the introduction of the Corniche – a super-luxury Swift model based on the Danette layout. With no green panels, the exterior was in a plain white with coach-lines to break up the side panels. Swift added a space gas heater, a full oven, fridge, Draylon upholstery, plus an auto-reverse system by Marwood. Underfloor insulation was included too, allowing the extended use of all Swift models in colder weather.

The Alouette name was re-introduced too by mid-1975, this time as a 16-foot family model in five/six berth, while the 1976 model year also saw another new Swift – a 12-foot 6-inch four berth named the Minuette. The Swift lower green waistband was smaller and placed in the centre of the side panel. While most of Swift's competitors had diversified into lower-end entry-level models, Swift continued to develop its mid-market models as

Midway through 1975, a new 16-foot six berth was added, reusing the Alouette name.

Swift introduced the Minuette, a 12-foot four berth, for 1976.

The Corniche 14/2 was introduced for couples after the 14/5's success.

well as its new luxury Corniche (Peters idea), which proved a best seller for the company; so much so that, by demand, the 1978 season saw a two-berth, 14-foot, end kitchen model join the five-berth layout. As fridges became the standard, the underfloor cool box didn't serve a purpose any more, and Swift would remove it after nearly a decade. Still using a Peak chassis, Swift now had these treated to stop rusting.

Swift's profile, which had become iconic among other manufacturers' ranges, was to continue to the end of the '70s. The 1979 standard Swift range was tweaked, with all windows being acrylic double-glazed units and a glazed stable door was now standard. Swift's Corniche range also now had a galvanised chassis and restyled front locker, a larger fridge and new reading lights. Swift's two ranges were very well specified for the prices, which ranged from £2,090 for the Minuette up to £3,157 for the top-of-the-range family Corniche.

Even though the UK touring caravan market had seen a tough few years, Swift, in comparison, had increased its market share. Now producing 1,500 tourers a year, and employing up to 140 staff, Swift had seen its production rise. With personal tragedies and some difficult years, Swift, with Peter firmly steering the company to further successes, would enter the next decade stronger than most of its competitors. The early 1980s forced

Above: The 1979 Swift range had double glazing added.

Left: The Swift factory had seen several expansions, including a new office block.

A Swift in production in 1979, prior to insulation and outer cladding being added.

many well-known caravan manufacturers out of business – even larger concerns such as Astral and the Ci Group, who produced the famous Sprite and Eccles ranges.

Peter Smith had kept the company going in testing times but had increased output and models and Swift's popularity. To quote Peter: 'I am sure our size and low overheads helped keep us in profit, and producing attractive well priced tourers that were also light and economical to tow kept up demand.' The 1980s would prove a decade of design innovation for Swift, as well as improved construction and new profiles. The '80s would also see Swift strengthen its portfolio with the acquisition of luxury coachbuilt tourer manufacturers Cotswold Coachcraft. The next decade would see Swift climb to be the third largest UK touring caravan manufacturer. Exciting times for the brand were firmly ahead.

CHAPTER THREE

The '80s: New Designs and Developments – 1980 to 1989

By the second half of 1980, the UK was in recession. Caravan sales were hit along with everything else, such as cars and general consumer products. Factories shut and unemployment was on the rise at a dramatic rate. This period saw several caravan manufacturers shut, including once big names such as Thomson. Peter Smith knew that to keep demand up for Swift tourers he would need to tempt would-be caravan buyers with new models while also providing more value. Swift decided to increase its luxury Corniche range, adding new models including the 16/6 – a large, family, luxury layout based on the Alouette in the standard Swift range. Items fitted in the 1980 Corniche included the Labcraft TP2, which offered the facility for mains electric conversion.

Swift's standard range saw in the new decade with a six-strong layout choice offering comfort and a specification that could be added too. The weights of Swifts had always been low for the type of market they were aimed at and this period continued that trend. Even the double dinette Alouette had a MIRO of just 864 kg while the high-spec Corniche range came in at 762 kg MIRO for the 13/2 end kitchen two berth. Peter was interested in designing a new generation of Swifts for the '80s. Employing wind tunnel testing, Swift

The recession of the early 1980s dealt a cruel blow to manufacturers such as Thomson, forcing them out of business. Swift, however, flourished. Pictured is the last of the once-popular Thomson touring range.

Above left: Swift carried on developing and updating. This is the first Swift Cottingham prototype built – a new departure for Swift in the late 1970s.

Above right: The finished Cottingham 440/4 had a smart new profile.

Right: Deep rear windows, a moulded roof spoiler and a lower back panel distinguished the Cottingham. These changes were brought about by wind tunnel tests.

were about to launch a prototype that would still retain Swift looks and yet have a modern, innovative, more aerodynamic profile. After exhaustive testing using the MIRA testing facilities, the new profile was finalised.

Naming the new design the Cottingham (after Cottingham village), the new model was a 14-foot 6-inch four berth complete with the usual Swift triple front windows, which had now been slightly raked back for added airflow. Sports wheels were added and the use of a rear moulded roof spoiler was implemented to aid the flow of air and reduce drag – a first on a mainstream tourer. The new model was built in the way that would later become the norm for most caravan producers, using sandwich-bonded construction for the sides. This method meant that the framework had polystyrene panels inserted, with the inner wall and outer aluminium then glued on, making a firm but lightweight construction.

The new Cottingham remained traditional inside but did have a more modern roof locker design, plus wrap-around front seating, and specification included a heater, fridge and a full oven. It was shown to dealers in September 1980 with production being implemented for the 1981 season. The Cottingham was a smart-looking tourer and was to be built on a galvanised chassis (which all the Swift ranges would now also use). By 1982 the Cottingham range had grown into three models, which included what would be Swift's first break into twin-axled tourers. The 550/5 offered the family of five a large, well-designed tourer with excellent towing qualities. It would also seal Swift's entry into the twin-axled market, being aimed at the caravanners who wanted larger tourers and with the new breed of 4x4 tow cars that could now tow them.

43

The interior of the Cottingham stuck to Swift's way of thinking.

A lawn show in 1981 with the two 1982 Cottinghams. Peter Smith instigated this central trade show in 1976.

The Cottingham 550/4 was Swift's first twin-axled tourer for 1982.

With three successful ranges, Swift were covering most of the UK market sector. From the 1970s, the 20,000 square feet of factory space had doubled by 1980 to more than 50,000 square feet to cope with the extra demand of production. The workforce was also to be increased, with advertisements in the local press for staff vacancies. From 1982 Swift fitted the Corniche with a mains inlet socket as parks began to add a few hook-up pitches catering for the new, more sophisticated touring caravan. Showers and more upmarket soft furnishings added to the luxury of the Swifts. The 1983 Cottingham rode on the latest Al-Ko chassis while the general Swift range came with improved storage and better-equipped washrooms. The Cottingham would also mark the first full-width end

Above left: Staff recruitment was carried out as the company expanded rapidly in the mid-1980s.

Above right: New buildings show the extended factory in the early '80s.

Right: The front lounge area of the 1982 Corniche 16/4. Access to mains electric was now standard.

45

Swift's 1981 Danette was one of best-selling models in its line-up.

washroom, two-berth model, the 440/2 – a layout that by the end of the decade would be popular in both two- and later four-berth formats.

Swift was seeing the demand for their tourers increase further, which meant that some of the models were sold out before the end of the season. Additional factory space was added and more land was purchased for future development. The Dunswell site had grown to 80,000 square feet and was now in danger of outgrowing its available land, so Peter purchased land further up Dunswell Road for use as another production area. Signs of the whole touring caravan market recovering, with strong sales after a downturn in previous years, began to appear around 1984.

Peter knew that improving Swifts with more modern and up-to-date designs would ensure brand loyalty. For 1983, the standard Swift range profile was given a slight facelift, creating a more modern-looking Swift, yet retaining the classic Swift profile. Swift was also involved with racing cars (sponsoring Ford's Formula Road Racing Team, for example), with such drivers as Dave Scott. It was also another way of promoting Swift as a brand of top touring caravans. In 1983 Peter had watched sales increase in the motorhome market, especially with coachbuilts. He saw this as the next step in Swift's brand development, with plans afoot for a prototype.

In 1983 a prototype coachbuilt motorhome would be built using a Mercedes 307D chassis cab. Utilising the Swift Cottingham profile, it was an overhead cab design capable of sleeping four persons. In fact, the prototype was named the Cottingham motorhome with the rear back panel and Cottingham name attached. This would be further developed over the next twelve months but motorhome manufacture wouldn't commence until 1985/6. Swift, in the meantime, were working on using GRP moulded units for their tourers and new aerodynamic designs were soon to be seen. Nearby rival ABI, in Beverley, had redesigned its Award luxury range for 1983, with demand outstripping supply.

Above left: The Swift range for 1983 had a slight facelift to update the profile.

Above right: Swift would be heavily involved with motor racing, and still is in 2018.

Right: Prototype building of a motorhome, seen in 1983.

Using a Mercedes 307D, the first Swift motorhome built was ready for evaluation.

47

The prototype used the Cottingham tourer mouldings and design.

In 1983, Swift, using their own GRP facilities, developed what would become the beginning of a new generation of Swift tourers. Further testing commenced with the knowledge that the public wanted a tourer that not only performed well on site and road, but also looked good being towed by the now-growing, aerodynamically designed family cars. Using Al-Ko suspension with a Syspal aluminium chassis, the new 1984 Corniche front end had two GRP mouldings with the lower section incorporating an air-dam. The rear was also a newly designed panel with integral road lights, while the sides had GRP wheel spats and side mouldings. Tested up to speeds of 100 mph, the Corniches were seen as being one of the most innovative tourers on the market.

Interiors were also upgraded but remained traditional in style and finish. Six layouts were now part of the Corniche range while the Cottingham received new wheel spats and GRP side skirts to further improve the airflow around the van. Mains access and upgraded furniture helped give the Cottingham more appeal. Swift's standard range also received the Syspal aluminium chassis with Al-Ko suspension, which was lowered to help reduce wind resistance. Interior changes were kept to a minimum but as part of the upgrade a Truma Space heater was now standard.

The days of employees delivering caravans in their spare time was long gone; now, Swift used various transport companies. One which proved ideal was Burstwick Freight, who from 1981 had begun to transport for Swift all over the UK. Burstwick would also deliver for other caravan and holiday home manufacturers but it was an ideal situation that Burstwick would become a member of the ever-expanding Swift Group in the mid-1980s. Burstwick also had a fleet of special-parts delivery vans to service Swift dealerships.

In just twenty years Swift had grown from a one-man family business to a major force in the UK caravan industry. Exports too played a large part and the Swift name was well-known in Europe.

Two years prior, in 1981, the Swift name had been applied to a motorhome, but more development was needed, and the motorhome production line was to be set up in a new factory area. In 1985 Swift had a busy year, as it would see the launch of their Kon-Tiki

New Corniche by Swift

When it lands on Stand 30, the amazing aerodynamics of this new super-Swift will be the big talking point of Earls Court 1983.

Corniche is already a classic but with new features and new fuel economy, thanks to its winning wind-tunnel styling, the new Corniche is certain to be a best-seller.

It's just one of the stars of Swift's new 'freedom' campaign to tempt thousands of families to fly the Swift way.

So don't miss it. You could claim hard cash just for looking it over! And you certainly can't overlook the new Corniche.

Swift CARAVANS

Swift's advertisement for the new, aerodynamic Corniche. Swift would build on their experience in modern tourer design.

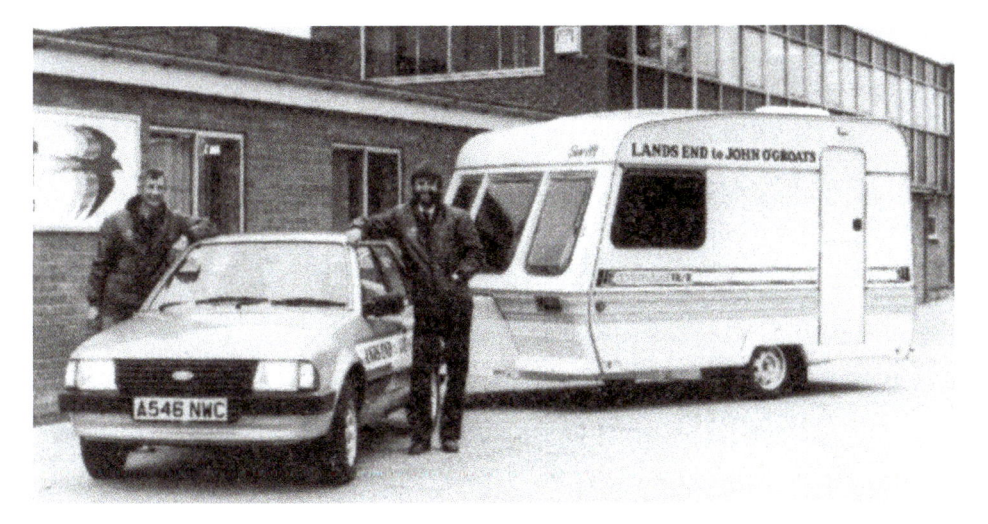

The new-look aerodynamic 1984 Corniche was towed from Lands End to John o' Groats – a journey of 876 miles that was completed in seventeen hours and fifty-four minutes.

Left: Burstwick Freight was to become part of the Swift Group by the mid-1980s.

Right: A new production area was set up to produce the Kon-Tiki and other motorhome ranges.

range of coachbuilt motorhomes. Combining Swift quality with style, the Kon-Tikis were a runaway success for Swift, with orders being taken over the next few years from Sweden, Holland and Denmark. Swift would soon establish themselves as a motorhome manufacturer.

Swift's design team had now brought another new tourer range to the fore. Named Challenger, it replaced the Cottingham range for 1985, though it borrowed the rear back panel from its sibling. The front was a new GRP moulded panel, which now had the gas locker integrated within the bodywork. Giving the new Challenger range a super front aerodynamic nose, three models were available on twin-axled, galvanised chassis. Testing was carried out on the new fully-equipped Challengers for stability and economy, with a test from Land's End to John o' Groats smashing a record previously set with a time of just seventeen hours and thirty-two minutes!

Corniches were also given more aerodynamic treatment with added radiused corners, but it would be 1986 that an integral front GRP locker and GRP roof would be used (another first for Swift), again pushing the aerodynamics further. Another Swift strength would be personal service; a key point Ken Smith had always tried to instigate no matter how large the company grew. Good after-sales service, which was also Peter Smith's priority, along with workshop seminars and factory visits, kept Swift in touch with its customer base too.

In 1985 Swift launched its official new motorhome range, the Kon-Tiki.

In 1985, the new super-aerodynamic Challengers replaced the Cottinghams.

In 1986 the company introduced Swift-branded clothing for a short while, including items such as jumpers, an umbrella and a Swift rallying jacket. This was all part of the forward thinking of after-sales service and brand awareness at the time. Swift dealers would be recognised for their service and sales with awards, which were presented by Peter Smith.

With a large owners club of well over 1,000 members, Swift had a loyal following. Many Swift owners had been with them from those very early Swifts just over twenty-one years previously. In fact, Swift sales had increased, with over 2,500 units being built annually by 1986. Factory space was running out and even more land purchases were made near what would be known as Gate 2, allowing production to increase further. The standard Swifts were now one of the most stylish ranges in the marketplace, borrowing the Challenger's overall look. Eight-strong, the Challengers ranged from the 390/2 at £5,695 up to £6,447 for the 600/4 twin-axled model.

The 550/5 and 520/4 have a rear bedroom with a sliding door for complete privacy (550/5 illustrated).

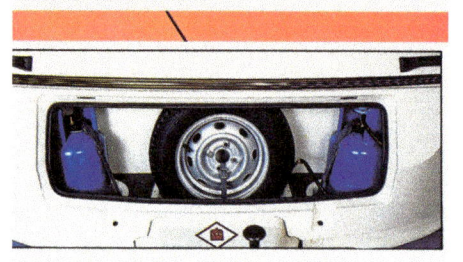

The integral bottle box has easy access.

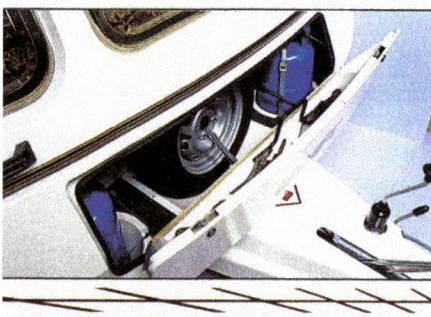

Swift move into the world of leisure fashion

Above: Swift's designer jackets and umbrellas were available in the mid-1980s.

Left: Challengers came with rear roof spoilers and integral front gas lockers.

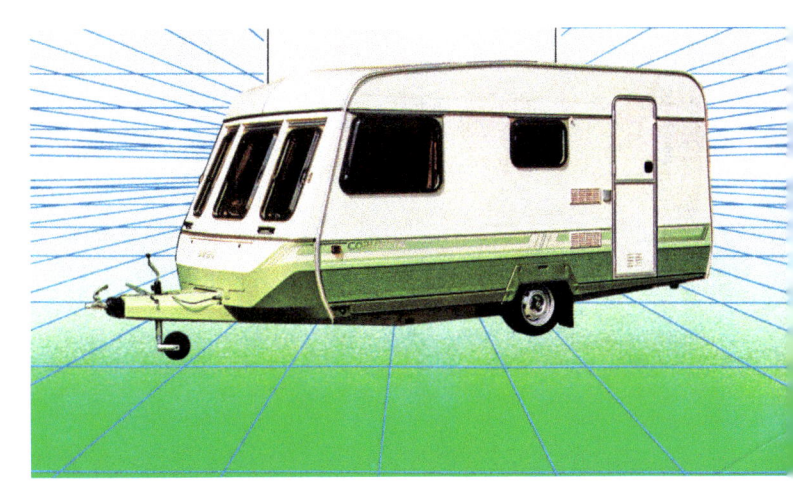

Above left: Swift dealer awards were presented for high sales; this was Broadlane Caravans' Colin Brown with Peter Smith in 1985.

Above right: By 1986, Swift's Ette range had the aerodynamic GRP front, borrowed from the Challenger.

Right: Swift's first entry-level tourer, the Rapide from 1987, used Swift's old 1985 profile.

The Limited Edition RAPIDE

THE RAPIDE

A body style that has an almost indefinable quality, standing up to the test of time so successfully that its appeal continues unabated. The values and traditions of this famous **Swift** style have been built up over many years, giving the highest quality and attention to detail our first priority.
In continuing with these traditions the **Rapide** will establish a new peak for others to aspire to and by introducing just two versions of the limited edition **Rapide**, Swift are able to offer a caravan which has a proven pedigree, at a price which is surprisingly inexpensive.

Up to this point, Swift had never ventured into the entry-level market sector. Back in the 1973 slowdown, makers such as Bailey, Avondale, Abbey and ABI would move in on Sprite's entry-level value-for-money tourers. This sector was popular with first-time buyers, but it wasn't explored by Swift; however, in late 1986 Swift would introduce its entry-level limited-edition Rapide (bringing back the name) into this sector. Two models at 12 foot 6 inches in length, using the original Swift profile last utilised in 1985, consisted of the 12/4 and the 12/2. A magnolia waistband replaced the original Swift green. Weighing just 641 kg MIRO and priced at £3,700 apiece, these two models became a range in their own right. Proving popular with first-time buyers, over the next few years a changed profile saw the Rapide as a competent entry-level range.

As the end of the decade approached Swift didn't rest on its laurels, and with the 1987 season the Challenger received an updated profile. Over nine models were in the line-up. The five-Swift range line-up now had mains electric fitted ready for sites that enabled it. Swift would also launch another name that would become connected with luxury and a high-end spec. This was the Conqueror, released in 1988 and the then biggest tourer in the UK, coming equipped on a twin axle with heating and air conditioning too. Short-lived, the name would resurface again in 1990 as a twin-axled range.

Now clearly the second largest manufacturer of tourers, Swift covered twenty-three models in 1988 and boasted the use of top-quality materials such as stainless steel screws for the exterior and 44-mm-thick Styrofoam flooring. New built-in flyscreens and blinds as well as solid ash-framed doors were added for Corniche, Challengers and Conqueror models. The twin-axled Challengers were now winterised using Alde ducted central heating systems, and also had on-board water tanks plus the latest Thetford Cassette flush toilet. Swifts now covered from entry-level to luxury, but 1989 would see their market sector stretched even further.

Since its inception in 1973, Cotswold Coachcraft had earned a reputation as a hand-built crafted tourer. Swift acquired Cotswold in early 1989 with a view to develop the brand over the next few years. Swift's design team hadn't been idle in the meantime, and had been working on the next-generation Corniche range, which was to take the touring caravan industry by storm. Swift used a GRP front panel and a one-piece moulded GRP roof and rear with a small storage boot, plus aerodynamic moulded side skirts and wheel spats finished in grey. Claimed to be 'the wind of change', the new Corniche looked to be a classic, aerodynamic design, and yet it retained its traditional interiors and a high specification. The Corniche was a stunner and an instant hit with buyers.

Meanwhile, Swift also updated its Challengers with an optional SE pack, and the twin-axled models now received two new layouts, including the new 560 with a large end washroom. The other six Swifts retained their 1988 look with just a few minor improvements being carried out inside. The 1989 model year was the company's twenty-fifth anniversary. To celebrate this fact, Swift included a Diamond edition – adding a shower, awning light, glazed stable door and a light in the front gas storage compartment – to its Ette range.

The Swift motorhome division was growing with the Kon-Tiki range being upgraded and extended from 1986. Using Fiat Ducato chassis cabs that were petrol to begin with, they had gone over to diesel units by the end of the 1980s. For 1989 Swift added another lower-cost motorhome range named Capri, which was another coachbuilt range that

In 1988 Swift launched its big, new, luxury Conqueror model, which was priced at £12,645. It was built for one year only.

The 1989 Corniche was a design breakthrough using GRP mouldings. It sold well over the coming years.

The wind of change.

1990 was Swift's twenty-fifth year so a Diamond edition of its Ette range was produced with extra spec.

Swift Motorhomes launched their lower-cost Capri range to attract more buyers to the Swift brand.

Manufacturing quality was stepped up in the 1980s.

By the end of the 1980s Swift had expanded and purchased more land for further factory space.

DESIGNED TO LAST

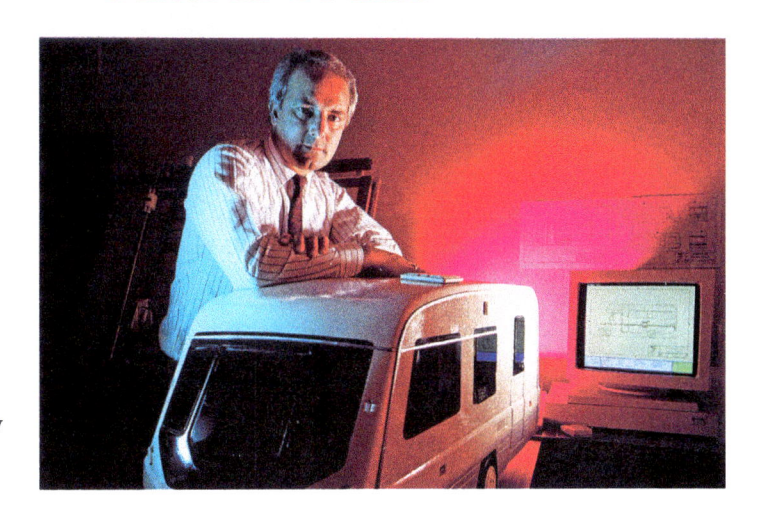

Swift's design teams constantly looked at new ideas in caravan design and interior decor.

would be extended by the '90s. Swift had, in a short time, established itself as a major UK motorhome producer.

With over 5,000 units produced annually by the end of the '80s and now with 500 staff, Swift's plants now totalled 212,000 square feet. By the next decade, Swift would acquire more famous caravan brands, making them the largest manufacturer in the UK. Peter Smith had developed the Swift brand as his father, Ken would have undoubtedly wanted to see the company grow. With investment in new computer-aided design (CAD) and manufacturing techniques, Swift's next ten years would see the company further increase its UK market share and lead the way in innovation and design. Peter Smith worked hands-on and the success of the company proved his natural ability to produce innovative tourers and motorhomes.

Chapter Four

Swift Expands its Brand Portfolio – 1990 to 1999

With Swift's market lead and now Cotswold under its wing, the company was set to expand even more. For 1990, Swift acquired an additional swathe of land of just over 5.3 acres near the Cottingham plant. The new complex to be built would also house a specialist after-sales spares department, which would ensure a supply of parts for all Swift tourers and motorhomes. Moreover, a purpose-built training centre for both Swift employees and dealership staff was created with the intention of keeping those who attended up-to-date with the latest Swift technology – another first in the caravan industry. At the same time, a new 12,000-square-foot building was erected in an effort to keep up with increasing motorhome sales.

After twenty-five years in business, 1990 was celebration time at Swift. The company decided to use a trade 1990 model launch for a two-day event, to which over 250 people came together, including directors and their wives dressed in '60s style clothes. Peter Smith presented long-serving employees and their spouses with special commemorative gifts. Peter also presented his mother and chairwoman, Joan Smith, wife of founder Ken Smith, with a special award. A firework display finished the evening off, making it a memorable twenty-fifth anniversary celebration. All new Swifts sold for 1990 came with a special 25th key fob, while a special anniversary logo badge was attached to each caravan to also help mark the occasion.

That year also saw Swift scoop awards from top-selling magazine *Practical Caravan* for Best Family Tourer and joint Best Family Washroom, proving that Swift's sound and practical designs were in tune with caravanners needs. In fact, this would be just one of many awards Swift's products would collect over the coming years.

Swift's involvement with CAD earlier in 1989 would influence the 1990 designs too. The new state-of-the-art computer design system could produce 3D drawings and complete shapes and components, cutting down time scales and improving accuracy in production too. This £500,000 investment allowed Swift a lead on not just UK competitors, but also on foreign tourer and motorhome manufacturers alike in the markets Swift exported to. Peter learnt that investing in the company produced better results as money invested always paid off with efficiency and design.

The Earls Court Show stand was also a showpiece of Swift's twenty-fifth year heritage; featuring polished logos, special clock towers and grey suede-covered offices, the result was eye-catching to visitors. It was the 1990 season that would also see the launch of the

Factory number two has since become the main factory and has expanded greatly since this picture in the early '90s.

NEW £300,000 TRAINING CENTRE IS A CARAVAN INDUSTRY FIRST

Swift built a new training centre for staff and dealers, which was a first in the caravan industry.

In 1990, Swift directors celebrated the company's twenty-fifth anniversary in true '60s style.

59

Above: Big celebrations were held in 1990; Peter Smith gives his mum, Joan, a special award for twenty-five years' service.

Left: A celebratory key fob was issued with each new Swift product sold in 1990.

Leading the field

Design, quality and choice are three of the main reasons that Swift has become one of the most successful touring caravan manufacturers in Britain this decade.

For the last 25 years the company has strived to produce a range of quality touring caravans that set the trend for others to follow. The 1990 model range is a fitting tribute to the company's silver anniversary and is the most comprehensive range ever produced under the Swift name.

Designs using the latest CAD CAM computer system to plan every element of the caravan down to the finest detail has made a vital contribution towards an eye catching range of new designs for 1990.

The Swift range leads the way with a new exterior shape and a new family model, the Baronette. The Challenger range has a completely new body shell, as have the four new twin axle Conqueror models. The Corniche styling has been further refined, giving it a pleasing, unique and modern appeal.

Investment in the latest technology for both designing caravans and controlling the very latest production machinery has enabled Swift to combine the best of modern technology with traditional skills.

Many of the component parts are manufactured on the main Swift complex in Cottingham to provide maximum quality control. These include the solid ash framed furniture doors, the fully insulated floors and walls, and the stylish glass fibre mouldings, which have become the hallmark of Swift design, combining eye catching exterior style with proven aerodynamic performance.

Swift models have many less obvious features which can make all the difference to holiday comfort, like the unique slatted bed boxes, which make access to storage easier and minimises condensation.

Swift used CAD to create more distinctive tourer and motorhome designs.

60

next-generation Swift Challenger range, with new profiles, updated interiors and better specification. The 1990 year would additionally see the Conqueror launched as a separate range. Being built onto an Al-Ko galvanised twin-axle chassis, the new range was equipped with a spec for all-year touring, making this range one that was undoubtedly designed for the serious caravanner.

With Swift's investment in quality, it shouldn't have been a surprise that the company produced as many of its components as possible, such as the GRP front and rear as well as roof-panel moulds. With such production facilities, Swift's factory floor space was 232,000 square feet by 1990, covering over 26 acres of land! In early 1990 Swift also brought all the Cotswold Caravan production over to the Cottingham factory with a view to implement new designs, which would happen for the 1991 season.

Above left: The new, revised 1990 Challengers offered more specification.

Above right: The Conqueror name reappeared for 1990 as a twin-axled luxury line-up of tourers.

Right: Swift's GRP division ensured that accuracy and quality was high.

The new Cotswolds were launched at the Earls Court Show in 1990 and re-branded as Swift Celestes. They now had bonded construction and a new shape, although this was heavily influenced by the original Cotswold profile. The Swift Celeste came as a two-berth layout with a specification that gave sheer luxury touring for couples. Swift had also decided to move the traditional front gas storage locker to the side of the new Celeste. However, it was decided after just one season the Celeste range was dropped after poor sales results.

Swift would unveil its new revamped entry-level Rapides at the following NEC 1991 February Caravan Show, which came complete with a new, modern profile while still retaining the light green side bands used on the Ette Swift range.

The new Rapide range now also had side gas locker mains electrics, better-quality interior furnishings and furniture, all while keeping prices competitive. Prices ranged from £5,895 for the 380/2 up to £6,895 for the 450/5. The new Rapides offered a value-for-money price and yet still retained the quality and style found on the more expensive Swift ranges. Swift was also making additional inroads into the motorhome market too, expanding the Kon-Tiki range while still using the Fiat Ducato base units that Swift would later add to the Capri range.

The Capris were added for those aspiring to enter Swift motorhome ownership and Swift also launched its Royale range a few years later, further enforcing their position as a number-one UK motorhome producer. At the 1991 Earls Court Show, Swift sold £1.5 million worth of motorhomes. Its touring caravan division exceeded £4.5 million, making the show a record-breaker for the company. Further enhancing this sales success, Swift received a large order for Scandinavia worth over £1 million in early 1992.

After just five years, Swift had become the number one-selling motorhome in Sweden as well as having new export opportunities in France. Its tourers were also selling into Denmark and Holland, where the Swift brand was well known and trusted; this was not surprising really, considering the amount of testing Swift products had to go through.

Left: The Swift Celeste was a super-luxury two-model range launched for 1991, but it had limited success.

Right: Swift's Rapide was updated for 1991 and proved a sales success.

Above left: Swift Rapide interiors echoed more expensive Swifts, representing excellent value.

Above right: Swift had further developed its Kon-Tiki range from 1990, growing its layouts and adding new profiles.

Right: The 1992 Swift Rapide 380/2 at Millbrook testing ground, which set a new twenty-four-hour speed record.

By the end of 1991 a new test system was put into force to ensure Swifts were tested to the limits and beyond that of a normal touring caravan. Safety and stability testing with speeds of over 80 mph was implemented with careful monitoring of components such as the brakes, bearings and tyres. Test simulating over 25,000 miles in less than twenty-four hours using rigs, rolling roads and test track facilities in Europe put the caravans through rigorous testing procedures. Testing new models ensured the caravans were built to last for many years. For the 1992 season, Swift broke two towing records during their testing programme. One was achieved at the Millbrook test track when chairman Peter Smith, a

News Release

VAUXHALL

VAUXHALL AND SWIFT AVERAGE OVER 97 MPH TO SET A NEW 24 HOUR SPEED RECORD

A Vauxhall Carlton 3.0i GSi 24v has set a new 24 hour national speed record for a car and caravan combination by averaging 97.04 mph at the Millbrook test track.

The outfit covered 2,328.97 miles in 24 hours of driving. Both car and caravan, a Swift Rapide 380/2, were standard showroom models with no engine or touring aid modifications.

The outfit was driven by Swift Group Executive Peter Smith, Sales Director Ron Shipp and caravan journalist Tony Bradford, who each took two hour stints at the wheel.

The team also smashed the existing record for 24 hours - including stops for servicing and petrol - of 77.44 mph set by Swift in 1984.

The Carlton and Swift Rapide outfit averaged 88.04 mph over 24 hours, including refuelling, covering a total of 2112.92 miles. Both records were scrutinised by official RAC timekeepers.

Caravans are currently restricted to 60 mph in the UK, and the record attempt was staged to prove the stability and safety margins of Swift caravans.

- more -

Vauxhall is backed by the worldwide resources of General Motors

Vauxhall Motors Limited
Griffin House PO Box 3 Luton LU1 3YT
Telephone 0582 21122

A Vauxhall press release on the record-breaking news.

caravan journalist and a fellow director, took a standard 1992 Swift Rapide 380/2 coupled up to a Vauxhall Carlton petrol engine 3-litre GSi twenty-four-valve saloon and covered 2,329 miles in twenty-four hours. Speeds of 100 mph plus and rock-steady 'take your hands off the wheel' stability was achieved.

The other record was set using a 1992 Swift Corniche 15/4 with a Vauxhall Cavalier SRi saloon car. The route was an 870-mile run starting at Lands End and arriving at John o' Groats fourteen hours and thirty-four minutes later. Average speeds set were 59.73 mph and, despite encountering dense fog in parts of Scotland, the run was a success. With this pedigree behind the Swift brand, one couple chose a new Swift Kon-Tiki 650/7 Turbo diesel with a full personalised specification to do a world tour, which would take them up to three years to complete. The couple picked the Kon-Tiki after owning one for several years and had trouble-free touring with it.

1992 was to see the Swift Group further expand its market, which in the last few years had been hit by a downturn in new caravan sales due to a recession that hit the early '90s. Competitors Abbey Caravans, south of the Humber in Grimsby, had seen its parent company, Cosalt PLC, with a heritage going back to 1966, invest in new models for this well-known name. In the summer of 1992, Peter Smith and the Swift Group purchased the stock and

Above left: Swift would acquire the Abbey brands from Cosalt in late 1992, moving production and design to the Cottingham plant.

Above right: The 1993 Swift range was redesigned and upgraded.

Right: By the mid-1990s Swift would build dealers special ranges based on standard Swift models – a very successful part of Swift today.

65

assets of the Abbey tourers. Production was moved over to Swift's modern complex in early 1993. The Abbey purchase would strengthen Swift's overall market share, while at the same time help develop the Abbey brand further. After sixteen years, the 2008 economic crash would witness Swift cut back ranges, with the Abbey name sadly being one to go.

Swift were set to push design limits further by 1993, with new profiles being introduced for the Swift Ette/Diamond range using sharper GRP front and rear mouldings and upgraded interiors. The Challenger SE range also had new smarter front and rear GRP panels and upgraded specifications while the Rapide was now known as the Rapide GXL range, which also had new-look front and rear GRP mouldings for 1993. Limited-edition models were launched along with dealer specials and by the end of the 1990s most large Swift dealers had an upgraded range made just for them.

An innovative idea for a large manufacturer such as Swift was the beginning of factory tours in this period, which would be a success for some years to come. By September, over 1,000 visitors had been around the Swift complex with trained personnel to see how Swifts were designed and built.

The Swift name was well known in Europe and Swift gave exports a further push for early 1994, designing a new range of four models for the Dutch market. Named Euroland, the range took Holland by storm, instantly attracting sales with this new-look Swift product, which had squarer lines than the Swifts marketed in the past. Interiors too were different, with light wood and a grey finish for the furniture along with more modern upholstery. For a short time, several UK dealers stocked the Euroland to sell on the home market too.

In 1994 it was celebration time again at Swift; the company had now notched up its thirtieth year. The Corniche range was to be further enhanced with a new profile using

Above: Swift designed the new Euroland range for the Dutch market in 1994.

Left: Interiors of the Euroland were contemporary and finished in grey wood, while layouts were in tune with Dutch buyers.

Above left: Swift celebrated their thirtieth year with three special Ette models based on the new Challenger profile.

Above right: Swift's first panel van conversion, a 1993 Carrera on the VW Transporter.

Right: In late 1994, Swift purchased Sprite Leisure and production would move to Hull from Newmarket. Pictured is a 1995 Sprite Major.

GRP bodywork mouldings, while interiors were given a higher spec plus a very traditional look consisting of brass handles for furniture along with new domestic-styled ovens and hobs. Swift also introduced a special Anniversary range consisting of three popular layouts. The specification was excellent and the profile would be based on the updated 1995 Challenger body shell. Swift had also entered the panel van conversion motorhome market with a VW Transporter as the base unit. The two-model Carrera came as either a two- or four-berth layout and was finished like a high-quality coachbuilt motorhome.

Swift had more news to announce in August 1994; continuing its desire to grab a further share of the touring caravan market, it purchased the Newmarket-based Sprite Leisure Group. This incorporated the famous brands Sprite, Eccles, Elite and Europa. The takeover gave Swift 30 per cent of the UK market, not to mention a greater market share abroad too. The famous names would come under a new brand name, Sterling Caravans, who would be allocated dealers of Swift tourers. The Sterling name would be successful but by 2018 was dropped, so Sterling Eccles became Swift Eccles.

By 1995 Swift would add what would become another popular Swift coachbuilt motorhome range – the Sundance. This was aimed at the entry-level motorhome sector and would prove one of the top-selling motorhomes in the UK. Swift extended its van conversions too, adding the Mondial – another name that would become well known in motorhome circles. Swift would launch special dealer motorhomes too, which were given different soft furnishings and exterior graphics and uprated specification, allowing dealers to have a range to their own plan. The idea would prove popular with other manufacturers, who followed Swift's lead.

In late 1995, a new warranty scheme offered three- to five-year cover on new tourers and motorhomes from the group. The new scheme was named Swift SuperSure Extended Warranty, and was introduced after a large financial investment into manufacturing quality a few years previously. By 1996 Swift re-introduced its Classic Ette range after an absence in

Left: The interior of the new Swift Sundance in 1996.

Below: Swift launched their SuperSure warranty across all Swift brands in 1995.

1995 with a range that had replaced them, which was named Azzura and was based on the 30th Anniversary specials. Swift looked at exterior GRP sides but decided to use this on the Abbey brand, originally starting off with just one model – the Abbey Domino 2.

1996 was to prove another important year in Swift's history. In late summer of that year Swift announced its purchase of another tourer brand, Bessacarr Caravans – a luxury manufacturer with a heritage stretching back to 1949. Swift bought all components and materials for the 1997 range and transferred production of Bessacarr from South Yorkshire to the Cottingham plant. Swift would develop the brand into motorhomes too, providing Bessacarr quality for the motorhome buyer. Swift's production portfolio now included Swift, Sprite, Eccles, Europa and Bessacarr, easily making Swift the number-one tourer and motorhome manufacturer in the UK.

Above: Swift's Ette models still sold well and were relaunched for 1996 after an absence of one season.

Right: The Bessacarr name was taken on by Swift for 1996; Swift would market the brand well in tourers and motorhomes.

A Swift being loaded into a container bound for Malaysia in 1996/7.

Over £3 million would be invested in 1997, including the construction of new offices, which also gave the design team dedicated new state-of-the-art computer-design technology as used in the car industry. New furniture-manufacturing techniques introducing computer-controlled machines with high accuracies in fit and finish were also added, along with extending tourer production lines and a new line being adding for Swift and Bessacarr motorhome manufacture. With over 100 layouts, the Swift design team were not only employed to satisfy UK needs, but also their growing export markets as far away as Japan and even Malaysia. Europe too was proving a growing export market, with Holland and Denmark being particularly strong customers for the Swift Challenger range.

Above left: The Dutch market proved successful for Swift's 1996 Challenger range.

Above right: The 1998 Corniche was another Swift classic, with luxury fittings and a distinctive exterior.

Left: 1998 saw the Swift Bel-Air A-Class motorhome launched. Unfortunately, it didn't catch the imagination of buyers.

Above left: The interior front lounge of the Bel-Air.

Above right: The Swift Gazelle would be sold on VWs as well as Fiats.

Below: By 1999, the Swift motorhome range had grown to five in thirteen years.

By the end of the '90s, the Swift badge was further catapulted to the forefront of tourer design. In 1998 the advanced design system would produce the stunning luxury-generation Corniche tourers, which would be sadly the last of the range. The profile added a new dimension to exterior touring caravan design, Swift design at its best, with the aerodynamic GRP panel's front and rear with flush fitting front windows. Interiors were given a new design with aircraft-style roof lockers and upgraded spec and soft furnishings. Swift had also launched its first A-Class motorhome, the Bel-Air, which was another class-leading motorhome from the Swift Group, although sales proved slow. By the following year Swift added another significant coachbuilt motorhome range, the Gazelle, which joined Swift's growing portfolio in the European motorhome market.

71

SWIFT SITE AT COTTINGHAM COVERS OVER 26 ACRES

Left: Swift's factory had grown considerably by the end of the 1990s.

Right: Swift launched their first UK-built fixed-bed layout for 1999 with the Challenger 500SE.

With an even larger share of the motorhome and touring caravan market by the end of the '90s, further expansion plans were put into force. Another vast investment of over £3 million was implemented into the Cottingham plants. More production lines were to be added to keep up with the ever-growing demand and more state-of-the-art design systems would be installed too. Within five years Swift had seen a 300 per cent increase in its sales, and the site had grown from 26 acres to 60 acres. Swift would also become the first major touring caravan/motorhome manufacturer to establish a website, which it did in late 1998. Furthermore, each new tourer/motorhome sold from the Swift Group also had a market research questionnaire included, asking the new owner to report on the dealer and the Swift product. This was yet another idea implemented as a first in the UK caravan industry.

With continuous development of Swift's ranges, Peter Smith had learnt from his father that quality, investment and customer care was behind the success of the Swift story. The last eighteen years had seen a break away from the more traditional Swift profile and with vast investment the Swift brand had seen massive strides, especially in the '90s. In 1999 Swift launched its first UK fixed-bed model – the Challenger 500SE. In fact, Swift were one of the first UK caravan manufacturers to produce this layout, which, within a few years, would become one of the most sought-after layouts in caravanning.

The new millennium would present new challenges and areas of growth too, with an opportunity for Swift to buy the touring ranges of one of its largest competitors. Swift were now not only the largest touring caravan manufacturer in the UK, but were also ranked in the top five in Europe as well.

Chapter Five

Expansion, Holiday Homes and Advances in Construction Technology – 2000 to 2018

The start of the millennium was to be another eventful decade for the Swift Group. There would be highs and a low as the first ten years progressed, with a mini boom in sales soon being followed with the global economic downturn at the end of 2008, resulting in some tough decisions taking place within Swift's brand line-up. But in line with continuing development of the Swift ranges, along with new European Standards including the prestigious ISO9001 certificate, Swift made sure it operated to the highest standards in the manufacturing process. This would help with exports to Europe as well, with this side of the buisness still being part of the Swift strategy.

The Swift line-up consisted of four ranges for the new millennium with revised and upgraded specifications. This model year also saw a choice of optional dinette seating arrangements too. L-shaped or full-wrap-around seating, or the standard parallel design, was offered to customers, enforcing Swift's commitment to customer satisfaction. Swift also fitted the new large Heki roof vents to all of its ranges for the 2000 model year.

By 2001 the Swift line-up was to see a new range, plus the deletion of the Swift Classic Ette range. In its place, the new range would be known as the Charisma. Offering more value than the long-running Classic Ette range, the Charisma came with a new GRP front panel and a new look with more modern graphics and interiors. The Charisma range proved a big hit with buyers, with its choice of family and couple's layouts.

In May 2001 it was announced that nearby competitor, ABI UK in Beverley, would stop tourer production. Originally known as Ace Caravans, they, like Swift, had struggled in the early days to get established. Ace, as with Swift, had become a well-respected name in the Hull area and then nationally from their initial start in 1962. By 1972 they had joined forces with Belmont Holiday Homes and formed Ace Belmont International. This gave the company a rating of the UK's second-largest tourer manufacturer behind the then Ci Group.

Touring ranges such as the ABI Award and Ace Jubilee were well respected among caravanners both at home and abroad. With the touring brands for sale, Peter Smith knew that these names would fit nicely into the Swift Group's portfolio. In the late summer of 2001, Peter announced that several ABI touring names had been acquired by Swift. These included the Adventurer, Award, Ace, Jubilee, Papillion, Monza, Sprinter, Manhattan and

Left: Swift developed new front L-shaped lounges, which customers could order instead of parallel seating.

Below left: Swift would press on with exports in the 2000s.

Below right: The Ette range would finally cease after thirty-five years, being replaced in 2001 with Charisma. Photographed is the Charisma 545 from 2003.

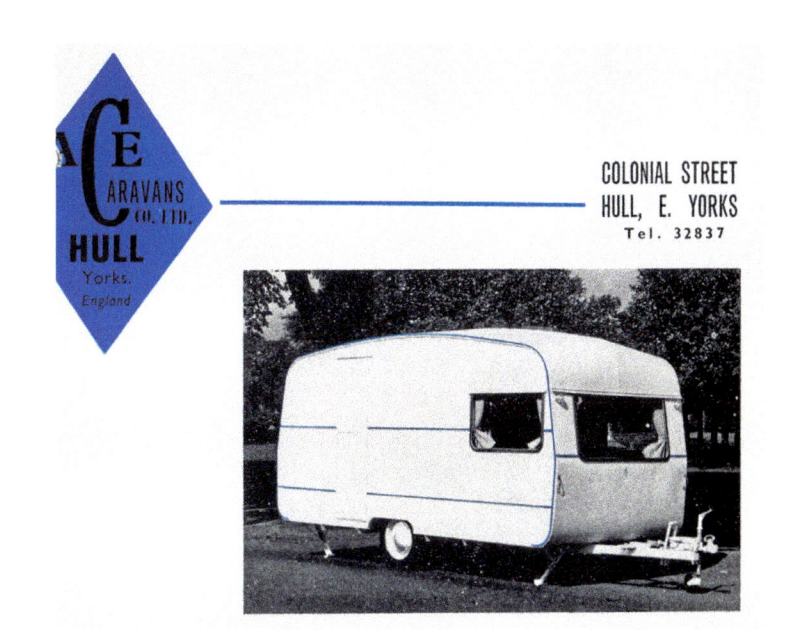

Ace Caravans began in 1962 in Hull, and became ABI in 1972.

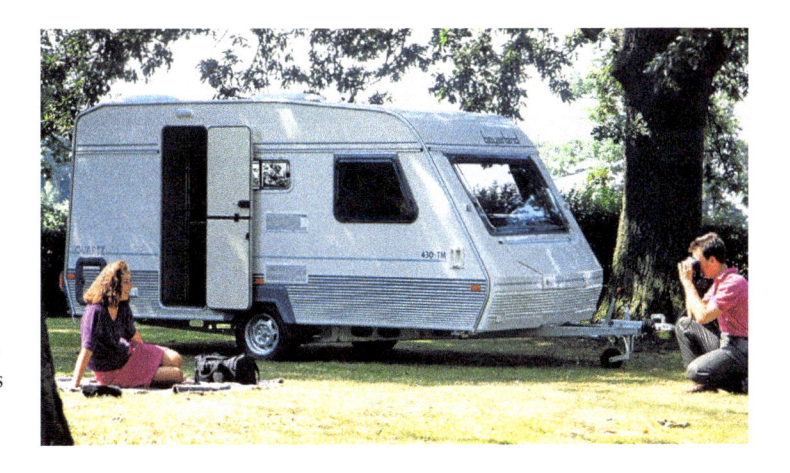

ABI exports were very successful, such as this early '90s Beyerland Quartz range.

the Brooklyn. Swift would expand its dealer network, taking on most of the old ABI tourer franchises. Swift's design teams went into overdrive with the plan to launch the Award and Ace Jubilee for the 2001 November Earls Court Show, thus bringing back the most popular names.

Based on Swift export designs, the new Swift-designed-and-built Ace and Awards were brought up to date and offered better value and quality of build over the replaced ABI versions. Swift's design and development teams were now involved with not only the Swift ranges, but also with the Europa, Eccles, Elite, Ace, Award and Bessacarr ranges, and from 1998 the Sprite as well, although this was for export only. Moreover, the motorhomes too were constantly being revised and kept up to date with all the latest design trends. By 2002, the Corniche was to be produced for the last time. As Peter said later, 'I created the Corniche and took the decision to finish it too.'

Swift-built Ace Jubilees were launched for 2002.

The Bessacarr interior. The Swift design teams had their work cut out for them in keeping ranges separate and improving them each year.

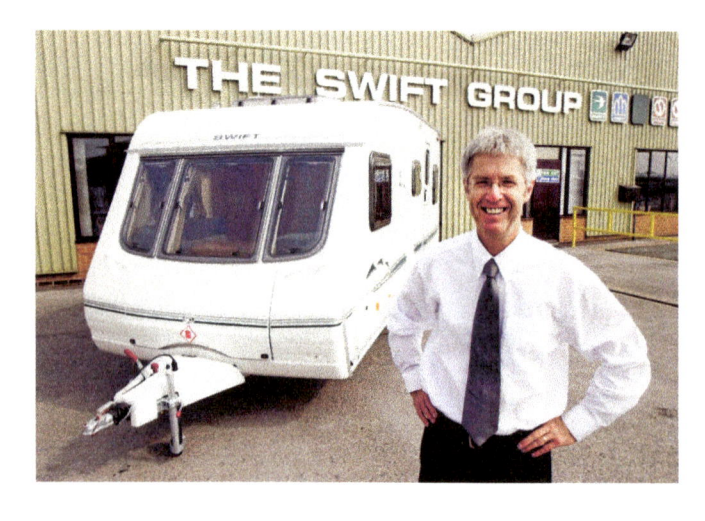

Peter Smith with the 2002 Swift Challenger. He decided to axe the Corniche in favour of the Bessacarr luxury brand.

Swift's constant improvement of its models would, by 2003, see some design features being incorporated that would make caravanning with a Swift even more pleasurable. New features included a first for a major tourer manufacturer. This was the fitting across all ranges of a duel fuel hob, which was also fitted on the Conqueror and Challengers. The following year, a new-design stainless steel sink bowl with a clip-on drainer and a chopping board was added on the Charismas – yet another innovative Swift idea. Other features included larger bed tops for easier access and a cantilever mechanism for easy lift-up operation.

One other notable feature was fitting the Al-Ko AKS 2004 hitch stabiliser, thus aiding towing stability. With the success of the fixed-bed layouts now available in all the Swift brands, a new family layout was added by 2004. This consisted of rear fixed full-width bunk beds, a side single dinette with a kitchen and a washroom opposite, plus a wardrobe and a large front lounge area. Named the Charisma 570, it would be another top seller for the Swift Group. For 2005, the Charisma would also receive a new twin-axled, six-berth, end washroom layout, which was named the 590. This would be the first twin axle on any standard Swift tourer range.

Right: Swifts had duel fuel hobs by 2003 and separate sinks with clip-on drainers by 2004.

Below: The Charisma six-berth 570 was a hit with families in 2004, coming with fixed bunk beds.

77

Interior of the Charisma 570, demonstrating the fixed rear beds.

Swift's first holiday home, the Vendee, was released for 2005.

The comfortable and upmarket lounge of the Vendee.

Big Swift news was on the way in 2004. Being a leading manufacturer of tourers and motorhomes, another market sector had until now been untapped by Swift, though it was naturally seen as the next opportunity: the holiday home market. Back in 2003, 30,000 holiday homes had been sold by UK manufacturers and Swift could become part of this market sector. Swift could have approached another holiday home maker but decided that this was a strictly Swift venture, which was to offer both the Swift stamp and the distinctive Swift feel. The decision was taken in February 2004 to enter this market but aiming for the higher end, with customer support being key. Within a six-month period, Swift had built several prototypes, which were then aired to several park owners and dealers, with the resulting comments provided then being taken onboard.

This new market sector also needed a fresh approach to construction and design. For example, by using a central roof beam running the length of the unit, wiring and ceiling mouldings could be neatly housed. With the main factory in full swing with tourers and motorhomes, another factory was needed to produce the holiday homes. The factory would be near Swift's original birthplace on Hedon Road. Within three months the factory was ready and the first units were coming off the production line. Typical of Swift's driven marketing and efficient production skills, the new homes had taken less than twelve months to design, prototype and then put into full mainstream production in June, ready for the 2005 launch season. The two models – the Debut and Vendee – were to prove top sellers and generated the growth of the further models Swift Holiday Homes would produce over the coming years.

The new homes were also given unique selling features in several areas. Firstly, due to the high construction and insulation qualities, they were designed to be used through all twelve months of the year, which was a priority for many users who wanted more from their investment. As well as the design of all the interiors, with contemporary overtones, the king-size beds, generous storage, chrome mixer taps, full-size ovens, domestic-quality mattresses and the opening double-glazed windows were intended to appeal to a large buying sector. For 2005, the first official model year, the aim of 1,000 units was the goal to achieve. Swift's management hadn't expected to have a run-away success; rather, it expected a slower pace, with new homes being steadily produced. Within a few years, Swift's new division had added the Moselle, Champagne and Chamonix, becoming a major force in the holiday home market.

By 2005 Swift developed its new locker construction system for its tourers and motorhomes, which were to be strong and durable while saving both weight and costs. All the internal roof locker dividing sections had originally been of plywood construction; however, Swift

Left: The 2005 Debut holiday home would also establish Swift as a holiday home manufacturer.

Right: The Debut interior with a central roof beam, which was a feature of the new homes.

Left: By 2006 the Moselle holiday home range was launched.

Right: The Swift Charisma features that were standard in 2005.

invested in plastic moulded sections, replacing the plywood dividers. This move proved to be weight saving as well as being stronger, and this new, innovative system was later widely copied by most other tourer manufacturers. Swift also added aluminium-framed double bed tops, which also proved both strong and lightweight. Furthermore, all Swifts were now equipped with alloy wheels, while the Challengers and Conquerors were given new-look graphics and sumptuous interiors. With radio and CD players fitted in the top ranges along with microwaves, Swift's tourers were proving very desirable to own.

With the additional brands, Swift was looking at increased demand on its production facilities. The original Dunswell site was to be sold and the second site expanded, with the erection of a brand new 126,000-square-foot factory intended for the production of both motorhomes and tourers. Not only would the new factory be erected, but a new access road would also be built on the east side of the factory to ease traffic on Dunswell Road onto the Beverley bypass. Work started in 2005 on the new production plant and it was opened in 2006 by MP Alan Johnson. The new plant proved more efficient, with improved quality control too. At a cost of over £6 million to build and equip, this was a major investment, but one which Swift required in order to keep up with demand and stay ahead of the competition. The 2005 model year would also see the Sprite brand relaunched for the UK market.

With improved production lines and a cleaner working environment, the new plant was the most modern of its kind in the UK. Swift's latest production plant also meant

Part of the new chassis floor assembly section in the 2006 extension.

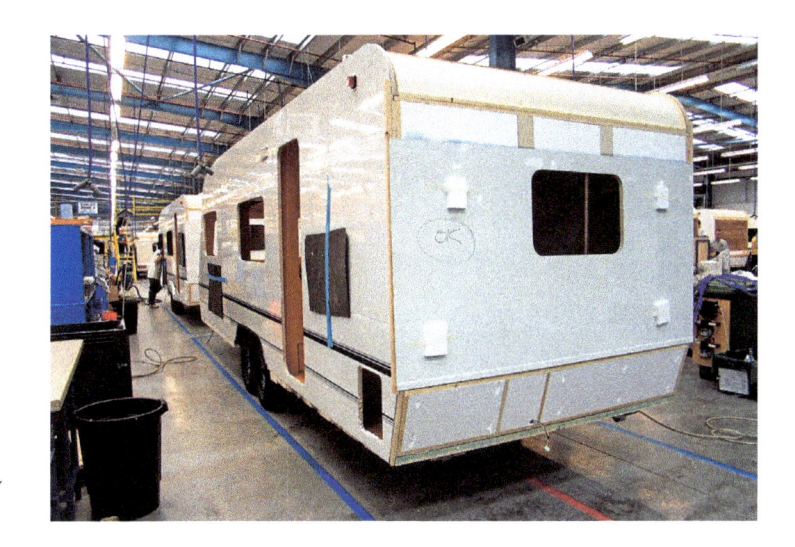

New production facilities allowed easy model changeovers.

Alan Johnson, MP for Hull, opened the new £6 million factory in 2006.

By 2005 Swift relaunched Sprite back onto the UK market after seven years.

Dutch-plated transporters loaded up with Swift and Sprite export models.

that higher tolerances and the ease of the ability to switch model runs quickly, including export ranges, gave Swift a clear advantage over its competitors. With over 900 staff – many having had twenty-plus years of service, who were always recognised with award presentations – Swift had built up a loyal workforce over the years. But customers were also loyal to the Swift brand, as one couple proved. Mr and Mrs McKenzie, who in 2006 purchased a new Swift Challenger 470, made it their twenty-first Swift tourer. This was a couple that just loved their Swifts!

Swift brought in new one-piece exterior aluminium sides for their tourers, which had a high-impact-resistant finish while enhancing the look of the vans at the same time. With the new improvements carried out over the years, sales of Swift products continued to rise. In 2007 both the NEC shows created over £41 million worth of sales. Over £10 million in motorhomes too were sold, which meant that, by the end of 2007, Swift's motorhome ranges accounted for 30 per cent of all new UK motorhomes sold. Still eager to grow, Swift was out to acquire another manufacturer, and this time it was to be a motorhome brand.

2007 saw the motorhome manufacturer Autocruise in South Yorkshire become part of the Swift Group. Manufacturing high-quality coachbuilts and panel vans, the Autocruise brand slotted in well with the rest of the Swift Group's motorhome ranges. The factory was maintained and Autocruise continued to be built at the plant. This year would also see a change in the Group's brands. The Bessacarr name would be dropped from the touring caravan division (a decision that was not taken lightly), but it would remain on the motorhomes.

However, a demand for Bessacarr tourers saw two dealerships commit to taking on the low production runs, basing them on the latest Swift Conquerors. Coupland would remain the only Bessacarr tourer dealership in the country, with sales still remaining high for these special super-luxury models.

Swift were proving again in 2008 how innovative a company they were. This time the Swift Conquerors were not only available in single-axled luxury layouts, but also with higher spec, including a Phantom anti-theft tracking system and Al-Ko wheel locks. The

The Al-Ko wheel secure was a Swift first; Peter Smith demonstrates it to onlookers.

Swift launched new silver-sided Elites and Conquerors, making them distinctive.

other feature would be the distinctive metallic silver sides, which were also used on the Sterling Elite and Conqueror ranges. This was yet another first for Swift, being the first major caravan producer in the UK to apply this type of finish. Alde heating was added too and all Swifts now had an exclusive moulded crockery storage unit, which kept most plates from moving when the caravan was in tow. The new microwaves that were fitted also had an exclusively designed plastic moulding unit integrated into the roof locker over the kitchen areas, further adding to the styling of the interior.

By the end of the decade, things were to change dramatically on a global economic scale, which would have a massive effect on the UK and European caravan, motorhome and holiday home industry. With the new 2009 models being launched, it was obvious by November 2008 that the recession had hit hard and, in an effort to downsize its portfolio, it was decided that some of the Swift Group's tourer and motorhome ranges would be removed. This would include the Abbey, Ace and Award ranges, as well as the Ace motorhomes. In an effort to concentrate on increasing the value of the rest of the Swift Group's brands, and to develop the other established ranges, this action was deemed necessary.

Swift would reduce its portfolio for early 2009 in order to concentrate on main brands.

However, the 2009 NEC show proved more successful than Swift could have imagined. Sales reached over £20 million, with higher-priced motorhomes proving a popular buy. This proved that Swift's marketing policy had proved right and that providing more value in the ranges encouraged new sales. With models such as the new single-axled, fixed-bed, full-width end washroom layout being expanded into the Charisma line-up, this was seen as a must-have for many couples, which kept interest high on the dealer forecourts.

With Swift's six-year warranty (which was later increased to ten years), as well as continued commitment to quality and further increasing its holiday home range, the group saw 2009's sales fare much better than initially expected. A new coachbuilt with Swift quality could now be had from as little as £30,000, seen through the introduction of such models as the Swift Escape coachbuilt entry-level motorhome. Coming on the Fiat Ducato chassis, specification included a shower, oven, and heating, as well as good storage facilities. Swift also relaunched its Mondial panel van range to much acclaim, and by the 2010 model year it had a fixed-bed layout included.

Swift would see further success at the NEC show in 2010, with over £22.5 million being taken in sales. Combined with the previous October show's figures, sales resulted in over £50 million – a fantastic achievement. This year would also see a milestone in Swift's charity

The Swift Escape was an entry-level coachbuilt range that became a UK best seller.

raising. From 1995 the company had raised over £45,430 for the Macmillan Cancer Charity, which was one of several charities Swift had helped over the company's history. Although Swift tourers were well insulated, the 2010 Swift tourers were put in cold chamber tests to test the caravans up to -15°C. This test showed just how well they performed, with the caravans achieving a Grade 111 classification – the highest grade achievable.

Also seen at this time was the beginning of another innovative idea – the Swift Talk website. The site encouraged all those interested in tourers, motorhomes and holiday homes to chat online and air their views on Swift or any other leisure vehicle manufacturer. With its foundations laid in late 2009, the site would become very successful, with clear indications that it contributed to increased sales.

When Swift entered the holiday home market just a few years previously, in 2005, the first steps into a new area for them proved a success, even though the holiday home market took a hit at the start of the recession. However, Swift's ability to design units as the market demanded saw them increase the models available, as well as continuing to improve the designs. Rigorous testing and customer feedback saw the holiday home division expand into Europe. Swift, as innovative as ever, decided to put into the construction of their homes the same bonded sides that were used on the group's touring caravans and motorhomes. From 2011 all Swift holiday homes had this new construction, making them very well insulated. Swift had also begun to look at the construction of its touring ranges. As a result, new, strong, redwood body and floor framing was given a liberal coating of anti-fungal and moisture treatment to add durability to the product.

Additionally, Swift had also been looking at tourer design over the last couple of years, and for the 2011 season introduced its new Conqueror, Challenger and Sterling Eccles and

The 2011 Swift Conqueror with its standard sunroof and new, sleek profile.

87

The 2011 Conqueror 480 interior was light and airy, with a modern locker design.

Elites. Taking touring caravan design to a new level using the latest CAD software, the new models were stunning both inside and out. The new models included a super aerodynamic curved front with sleek mouldings and a sunroof (then optional on the Eccles and Challenger), plus smart graphics and new full-height mouldings on the rear. The interiors included cream kitchen roof locker doors and new granite sink designs.

The specification on the Conqueror was also impressive, adding appeal to those buyers wanting a top-of-the-range tourer. Sales for the 2011 re-vamped models doubled, with over 110,000 enquirers alone before they were available on dealers' forecourts. For 2011 another milestone was reached, concerning the Swift Owners Club. It would mark the club's fortieth year, with a special rally being held close to the original first meet back in August 1971, near Alton Towers.

The success of the upmarket Swift ranges was to influence the next phase in Swift's touring ranges. A major redevelopment took place for 2012 of the other Swift, Sprite and

2012 Swifts under wraps at a Swift dealer launch at Willerby.

The 2012 Challenger Sports wowed with its profile. A sunroof was an option but was standard fit by the following year.

Sprites were to be known as Swift Sprites by 2012.

Sterling models. The new Swift look was to be applied to the two new ranges, though the use of simpler mouldings and both the Europa and Charisma would be replaced with the new ranges. The Eccles became the Eccles Sport while the Swifts were named Challenger Sports. Saving weight and improving specification as well as offering the most stylish-looking tourers in their price sector saw sales increase over the models they replaced. Sunroofs were classed as options but these were to be made standard fit by 2013 due to customer demand.

   The Eccles ranges had more contemporary interior finishes than the Challenger Sports, which still had a modern ambience but displayed a more traditional wood finish. 2012 would also see Sprites receive a major redesign; again influenced by the new Swift look, the Sprites were to offer style at an entry-level price. Furthermore, now known as the Swift Sprite range, the Swift badge was added to the Sprite, giving it a stronger family tie to the brand in general.

   By 2013 the Swift ranges had defied the downturn in sales of new motorhomes, tourers and holiday homes. Working hard to produce exciting designs and adding specification, including solar roof panels and sunroofs as standard, plus adding SE versions to both the

SWIFT TV

See product videos · developments and interviews at **swifttv.co.uk**

US ONLINE
twork for Caravan Enthusiasts
IFT-TALK.CO.UK

Swift TV was an innovative social media idea that would increase sales of the Swift product.

Eccles and Challenger Sports, saw demand for these ranges exceed expectations. With all of Swift's expertise in testing and design, all products now had European Type Approval, and all the while Swift's designers were working at looking at new construction methods in an effort to improve the tourers' durability, which would be unveiled for the 2014 range of models.

In the meantime, plans were put into place to move the production of holiday homes to Cottingham. Meanwhile, motorhome production would be moved from the Cottingham plant to the Autocruise factory in South Yorkshire. This would bring all motorhome production to one location, making it more efficient in the process. Swift's social media website, Swift Talk, had by 2012 topped 7,000 members, such was its popularity. The site was also used to highlight special 'dealer events', wherein Swift products were on display at promotional weekends. Swift would also work on another first in the caravan industry – its own online television station, known as Swift TV, where all the latest news and behind-the-scenes happenings at the group could be seen.

Over the years, Swift's motorhomes had seen great advancements in their design and build from that very first prototype in 1983. By 2013, low-profile models from the Bessacarr and Swift Bolero ranges boosted sales in this sector, especially with the inclusion of Alde heating and a Tracker system, plus added specification. While the entry-level Escape had more enhanced looks, the Sundance range was given a new look and higher specification, yet retained an affordable price tag. Swift's holiday homes were also launched into the residential market, with its Champagne Lodge being priced at just over £64,000.

Swift's design team always look for the latest trends in design, both inside and out. At the NEC 2013 show, the company put on display a prototype Swift named, aptly, the Concept. Although relatively conventional, and trading on the Swift new looks, the interior was completely contemporary, with a cream furniture finish, modern soft furnishings, rugs and new mood lighting, plus patterned interior walls. The response gave a clear indication that this had potential. After a survey of over 600 forms, the design team went away and

Swift's Concept tourer at the 2013 NEC show.

began to develop a new range based on the Concept prototype. Later in 2013, these new tourers would receive their first public airing.

It would be 2014 – Swift's fiftieth year in business – that the group was to launch two innovations in touring caravans. First of all, the construction of the group's tourers and motorhomes was to be radically changed. The bodywork would be wood free and in fact used Pure – a tough polyurethane material that won't absorb moisture. Named SMART, the new technology enabled Swift to keep stylish profiles while keeping weight down too. Fully

2014 was Swift's fiftieth year – Peter Smith stands with the new SMART-construction Elegance and Continentals that were launched that year.

tested at Millbrook, plus undergoing a cold chamber test, the new construction proved its worth in all regards. It showed a further commitment to the quality Swift customers both old and new had come to expect. The new construction was an advancement in touring caravan design and would add durability to the customer's investment in a Swift tourer or motorhome.

The latest construction was big news indeed, as Swift's advanced design team had taken the Concept's principles and put them into the Eccles Sport and Sport SE ranges. Bold exterior graphics and a matt black front moulded panel gave the new Eccles an attractive profile. Interiors followed the Swift Concept, with a white furniture finish and chrome inlays, while mood lighting added to the wow factor. Swift would also use the Duvalay lightweight memory foam mattress for its double bed. The mattress was deigned to offer maximum comfort while also being lightweight. The Duvalay Company had featured in the BBC Two television series *Dragons Den*, winning finance from Hilary Devey. Swift's design team saw the advantages of the new mattress and they became exclusively fitted to the Swift Group's leisure vehicles.

2017 saw Swift's Basecamp rear-entrance-door tourer take the industry by storm.

Fifty years separate the 1964 Ten and 2014 Challenger Sport.

A new Swift holiday home leaves the new £8 million Cottingham complex on 14 June 2017.

With a successful fifty years behind them, Swift's ethos had seen the best possible unit being made for the money. Making after-sales a priority alongside quality and up-to-the-minute designs would keep Swift ahead of the competition abroad as well as at home. At the time of writing, Swift have export markets in Holland, Belgium, Denmark, Australia, New Zealand, Germany and France too. Swift would win a large £5.5 million order for four of its holiday home ranges from a national park owner, while orders overall for Swift motorhomes and tourers had again increased for the 2014 model year.

With fifty years of progress and innovation, the Swift caravan has become a well-known name abroad as well as in the UK. When Ken Smith, along with his wife Joan, began making caravans in that small workshop back in Hull fifty years ago, they could not have dreamt that the business would have grown to over 70 acres in size by 2018, or that the company would still be around half a century later.

The new Elegance and Continental ranges were launched at the 2014 NEC show with new construction and highly innovative and specified models. Swift would further develop its ranges and increase its market share, and a new factory extension is planned for the summer of 2018 to consolidate all holiday home and lodge manufacturing to the Dunswell Road site. Sales of Swift ranges saw waiting lists and models sell out, and new management structures plus further heavy investment on machinery and advances on export markets have also been seen. The company also expanded its holiday homes, and by 2017 its super-luxury lodge, the Whistler, was launched at the NEC Show. Swift continue to grow and launch successful ranges that win awards in various quarters.

For 2017 Swift launched its funky rear-entry-door Basecamp tourer, hoping to see it sell a few hundred units; in fact, it has sold double that amount! Swift's Sterling range of tourers was deleted but the famous Eccles name now continues as the Swift Eccles and the Swift Sprite. A tie-up with US brand Airstream was also implemented in 2017. Swift's rallying heritage continues with their own rally car, a Ford Fiesta R, which again promotes the Swift Company. Over the years the Swift logo has changed, and the company has freshened up its famous badge for the 2018 model year.

Ken Smith would have been very proud but probably wouldn't believe that his one caravan back in 1964 would ultimately lead to the biggest manufacturer of leisure vehicles in the UK. The Swift story continues...